M000112475

Nudes
Index I

Bonner Straße 126
D-50968 Köln

Layout and Typesetting:	e-design, Bonn
Project Management:	Monika Bergmann
Production:	Mark Voges
Reproductions:	litho niemann und m. steggemann GmbH, Oldenburg
Printed and Bound by:	Mladinska Knjiga, Lubljana

Printed in Slowenia
ISBN 3-8290-0502-4

10 9 8 7 6 5 4 3 2 1

Nudes
Index I

Edited by Peter Feierabend

Introduction

This volume from the Index books series is dedicated to the classical genre of human nude portraiture. From Antiquity to the present day, artists have used this motif to practice and improve their technique and to match their skills against their peers. In Nudes Index I, the most diverse styles in the medium of photography have been used to showcase the human body. All works have had to meet the criteria of high artistic standards, and originality of content and technique.

The result is an exemplary collection of artistic responses to the challenge of a subject that is rich in tradition and balanced between private and public spheres. Within these qualitative boundaries, this genre covers a broad spectrum — from the classical approach and author photography to conceptional nude photography. The extraordinary techniques and perspectives on the human body displayed in these pictures will captivate readers; unusual details will require them to take a second look; thought-provoking essays will encourage them to peruse this book again and again; and abstract designs will allow their imaginations to run wild.

Nudes Index I is an excellent reference book for all those who have a special interest in contemporary photography, whether they are photographers themselves or just passionate collectors. A detailed list of addresses in the appendix of this book provides readers with the opportunity to contact individual photographers in person.

Vorwort

Der vorliegende Band aus der Reihe der Index-Bücher ist dem klassischen Genre menschlicher Aktdarstellung gewidmet. An diesem Objekt haben sich alle Künstler – von der Antike bis heute – geschult und aneinander gemessen. Im Nudes Index I wird der Körper mit verschiedensten Möglichkeiten des Mediums Fotografie in Szene gesetzt. Alle Arbeiten mußten sich dem Kriterium des künstlerischen Anspruchs sowie der inhaltlichen und technischen Originalität der Bilder stellen.

Entstanden ist eine repräsentative Sammlung von künstlerischen Antworten auf die Herausforderung eines traditionsreichen Sujets, das zwischen Intimität und Öffentlichkeit balanciert. Innerhalb dieser qualitativen Grenzziehung breitet sich das weite Spektrum dieses Genres aus: vom klassischen Ansatz über Autorenfotografie bis hin zu konzeptioneller Aktfotografie. Die Bilder betören durch außergewöhnliche Techniken und Perspektiven auf den nackten Körper, ungewohnte Details fordern einen zweiten Blick, kritische Installationen provozieren zum erneuten Hinschauen, abstrakte Schemen überlassen der Phantasie das Feld.

Mit dem Nudes Index I ist ein Nachschlagewerk für all jene entstanden, die ein besonderes Interesse an zeitgenössischer Fotografie haben, sei es aus beruflichen Gründen oder aus Sammelleidenschaft. Die detaillierten Adressen im Anhang des Buches geben allen Interessierten die Möglichkeit, Kontakt zu den einzelnen Fotografen aufzunehmen.

Préface

Ce volume de la série des Index est consacré à ce genre classique qu'est la représentation du nu humain. De l'Antiquité à nos jours, le nu a été un objet d'étude auquel se sont mésuré tous les artistes. Dans Nudes Index I, le corps humain est mis en scène avec les moyens photographiques les plus divers. Toutes ces œuvres répondent aux critères d'une haute exigence artistique associée à l'originalité du contenu et de la technique.

Nudes Index I présente des réponses d'artistes contemporains, nées de la confrontation à un sujet riche en tradition, en équilibre entre intimité et exhibition. Sans jamais déroger aux impératifs de qualité, un vaste éventail de réalisations se déploie ici : de l'approche classique à la photo de nu conceptuelle, en passant par les clichés d'auteur. Plusieurs photographies envoûtent par des techniques et des perspectives du corps humain hors du commun, certains détails insolites exigent un second regard, des installations critiques appellent à une observation plus approfondie tandis que certaines formes abstraites laissent le champ libre à l'imagination.

Nudes Index I est un ouvrage de référence destiné à tous ceux qui s'intéressent à la photographie contemporaine, que ce soit pour des raisons professionnelles ou par pure passion. Les adresses qui figurent à la fin de l'ouvrage permettent à tous ceux qui le souhaitent de prendre contact avec les différents photographes.

Prólogo

El presente volumen de la serie Index está dedicado al género clásico de la representación del desnudo humano. Todos los artistas –desde la Antigüedad hasta nuestros días– se han basado en este tema y con él han ido demostrando su valía consecutivamente. En Nudes Index I se pone en escena el cuerpo humano con las más diversas posibilidades del medio fotográfico. Todos los trabajos han tenido que someterse a criterios de exigencia artística y de originalidad de contenido y técnica de imágenes.

El resultado es una colección representativa de respuestas artísticas al desafío de un tema eminentemente tradicional que oscila entre lo íntimo y lo público. Dentro de esos límites cualitativos se extiende un amplio espectro de este género: desde el enfoque clásico, pasando por la fotografía de autor, hasta llegar al desnudo conceptual. Las imágenes fascinan por las in sólitas técnicas y perspectivas del cuerpo humano, detalles inusuales estimulan a una segunda mirada, instalaciones críticas suscitan una renovada contemplación y esquemas abstractos hacen volar la fantasía.

Con Nudes Index I ha surgido una obra de consulta para todos aquellos que tienen un interés especial por la fotografía, ya sea por motivos profesionales o por pasión coleccionista. Las direcciones que se indican en el Apéndice del libro proporcionan a todos los interesados la posibilidad de entrar en contacto con los distintos fotógrafos.

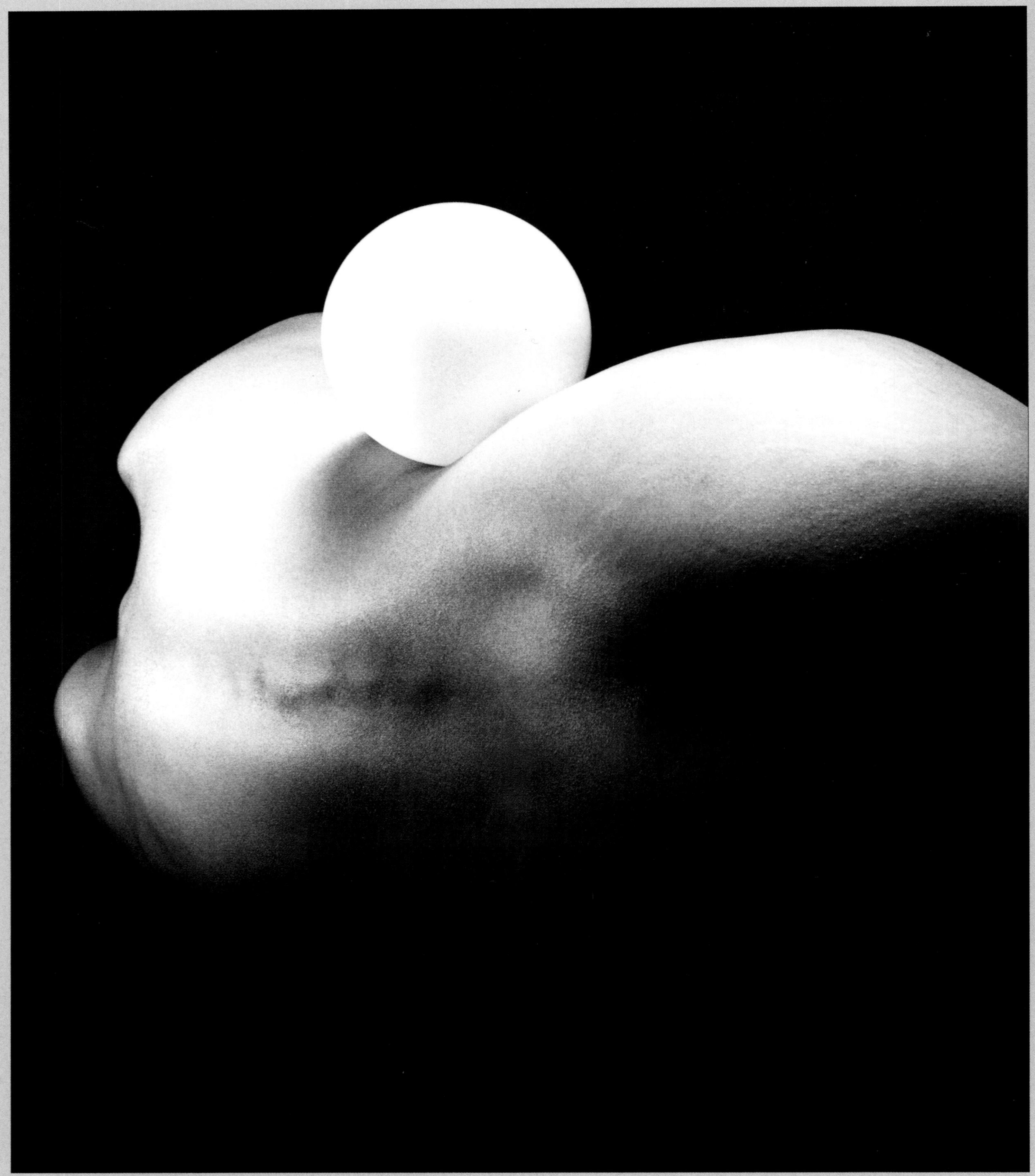

FEMALE I

◂◂ Günter Glücklich

Archie Kent

Robert Goshgarian

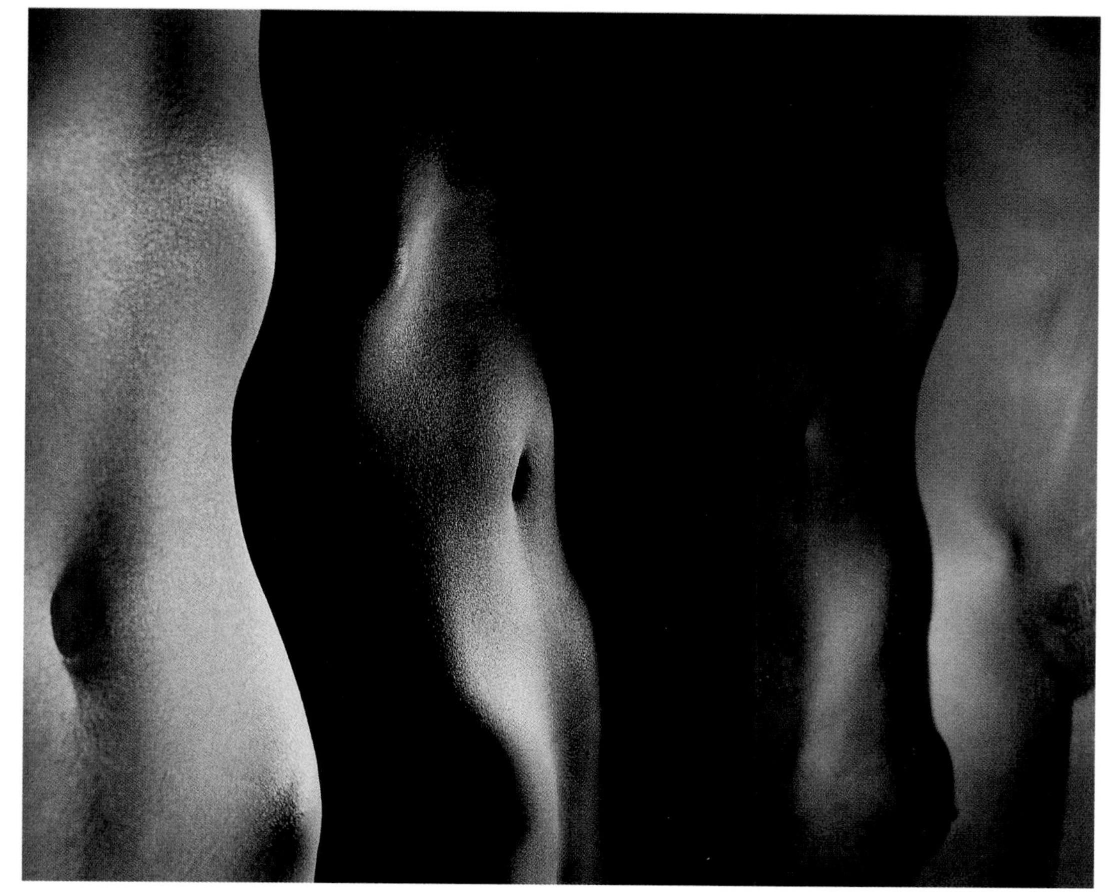

Josef Šnobl

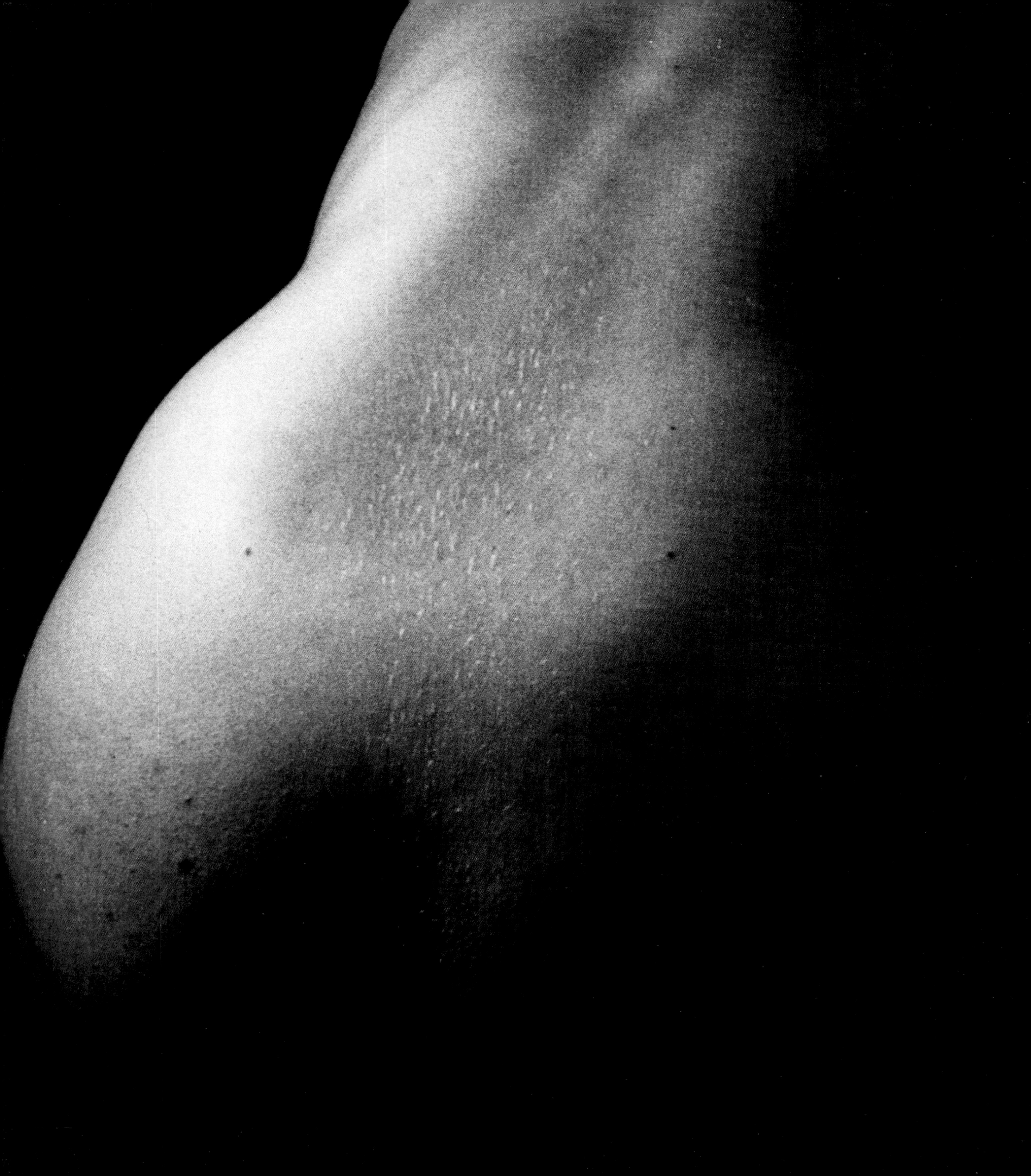

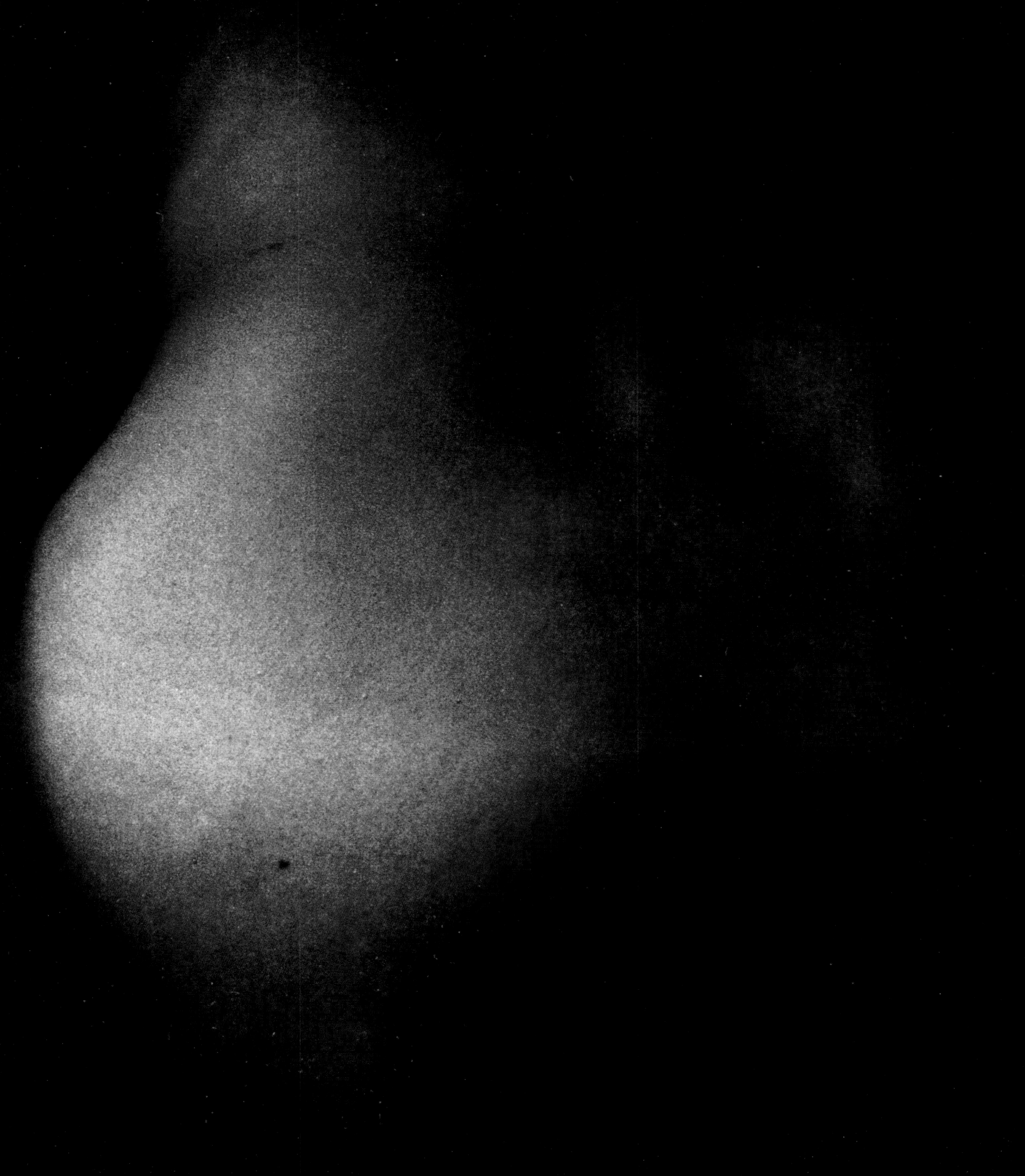

Yuri Dojc

◀◀ Josef Šnobl

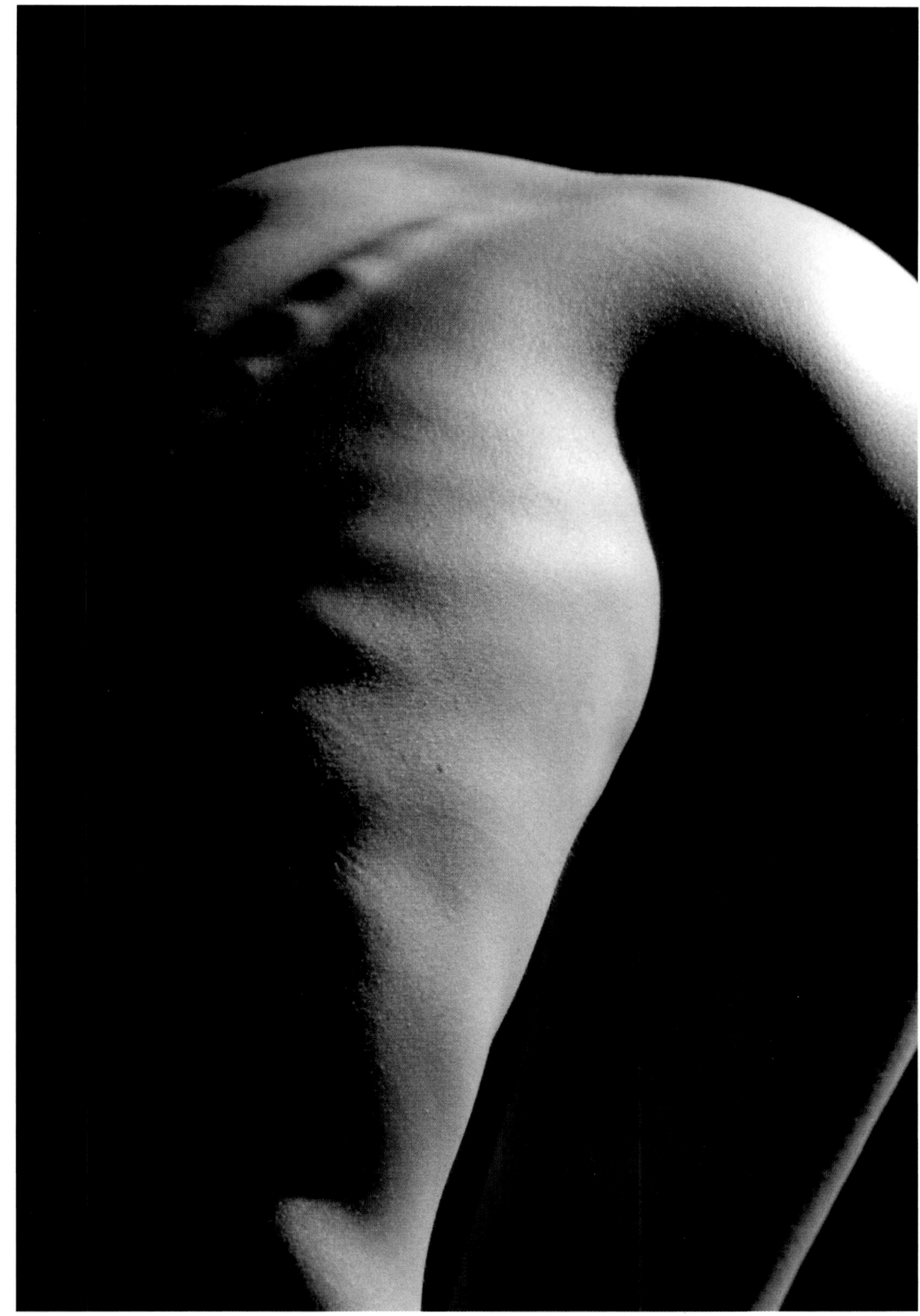

Pascal Baetens

Stephan Hederich

Thomas Schlömann

◀◀ Manfred Kötter

Mark Smith

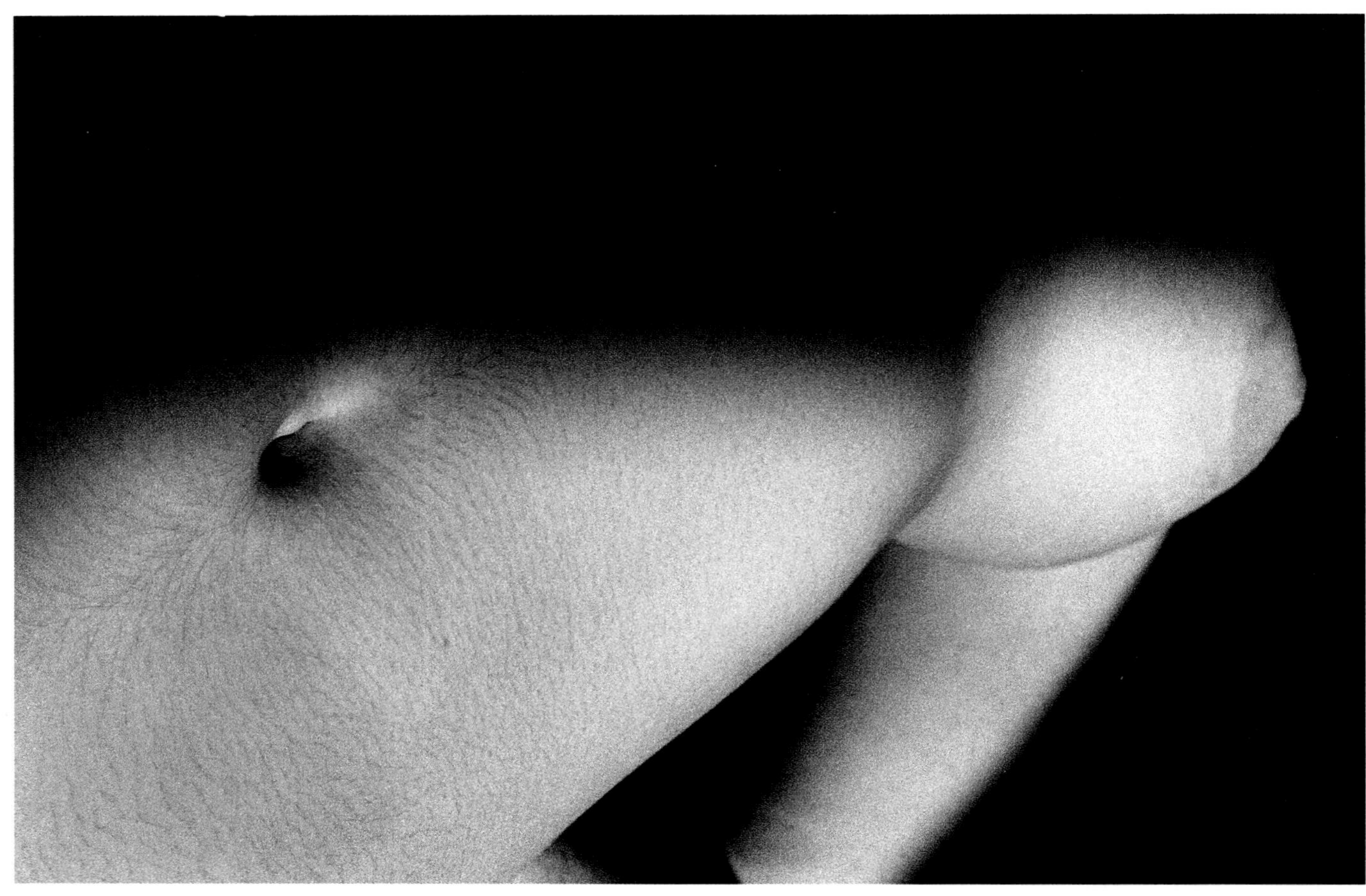

Arnold Crane

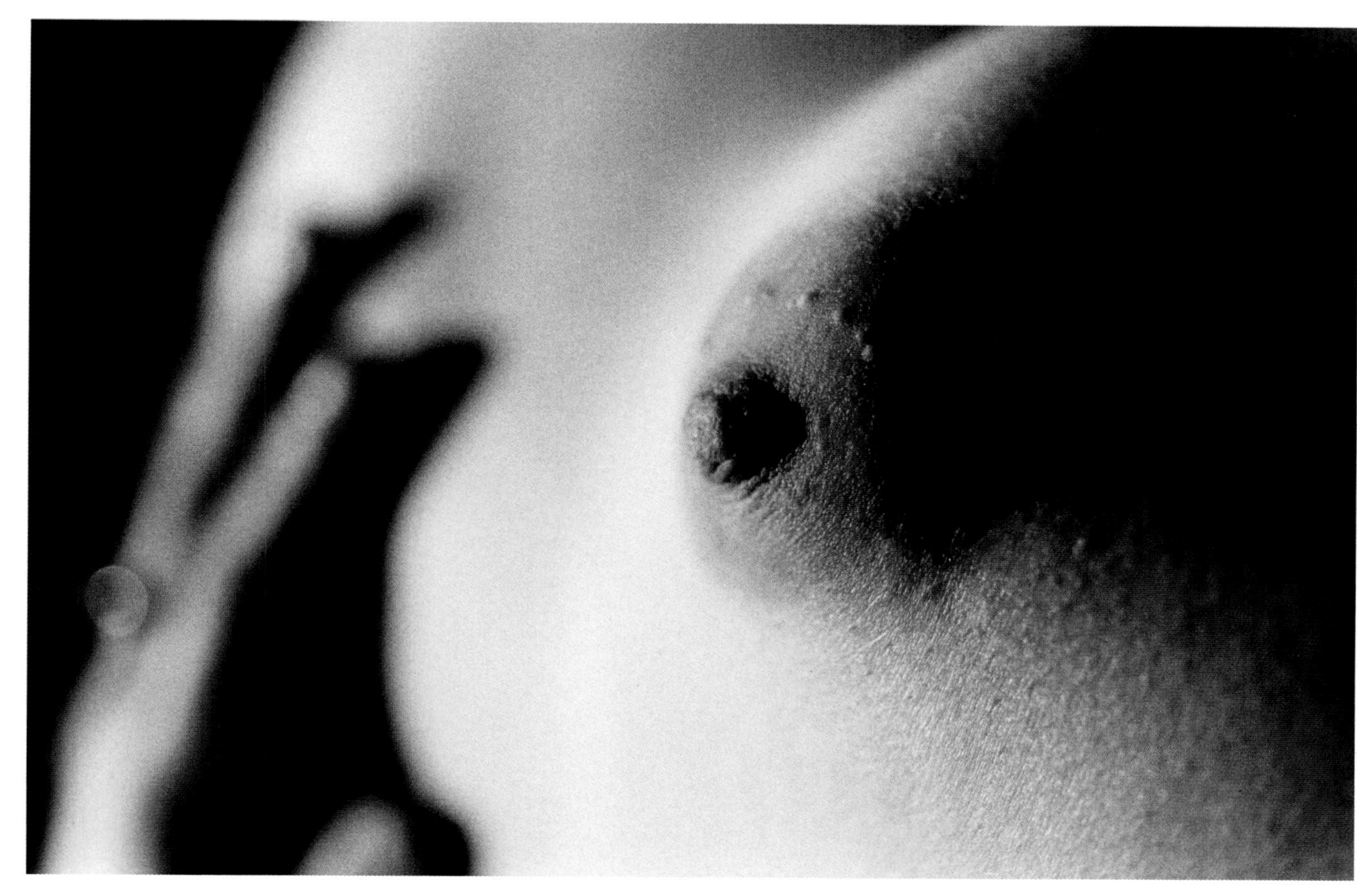

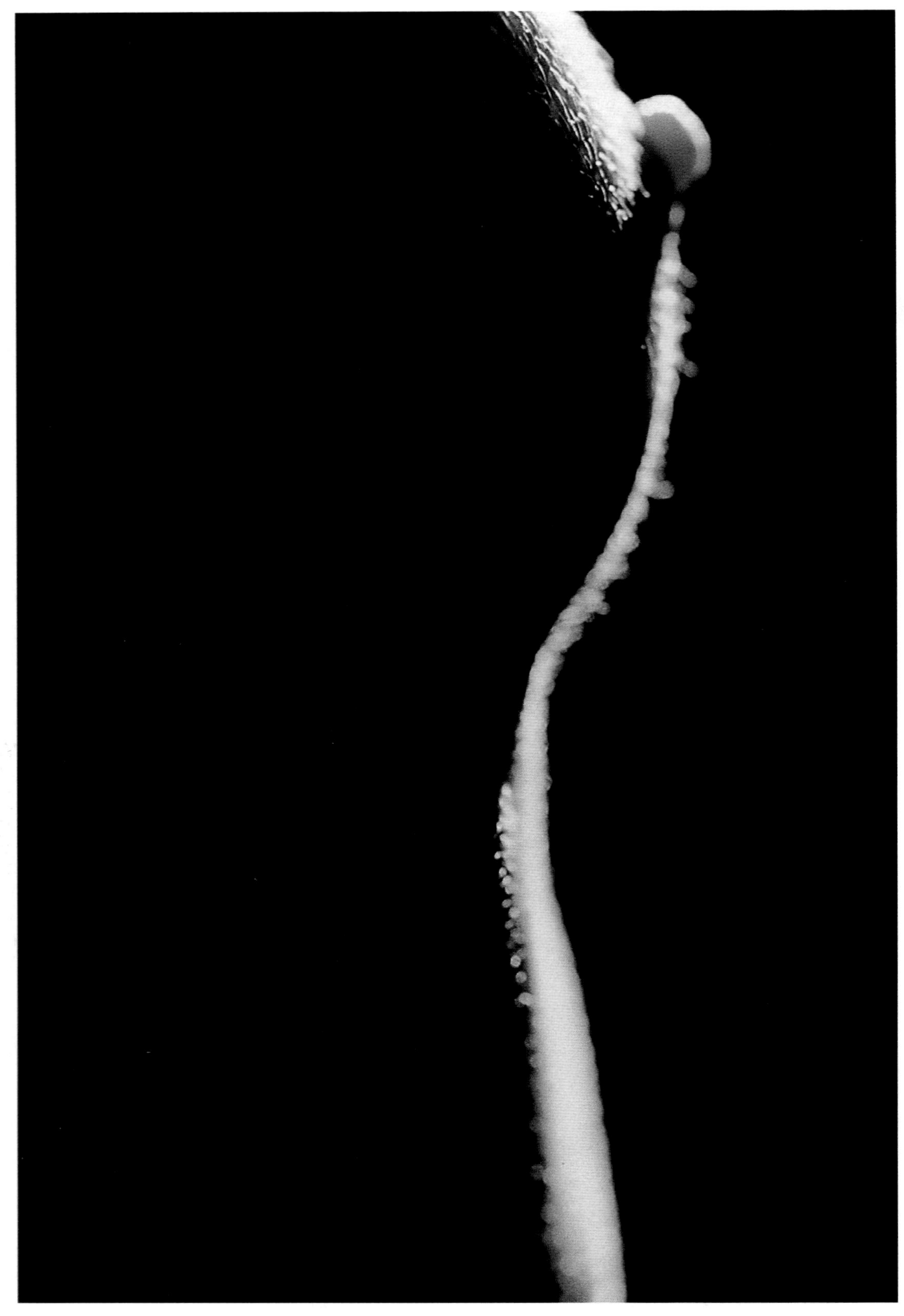

Rafael Navarro

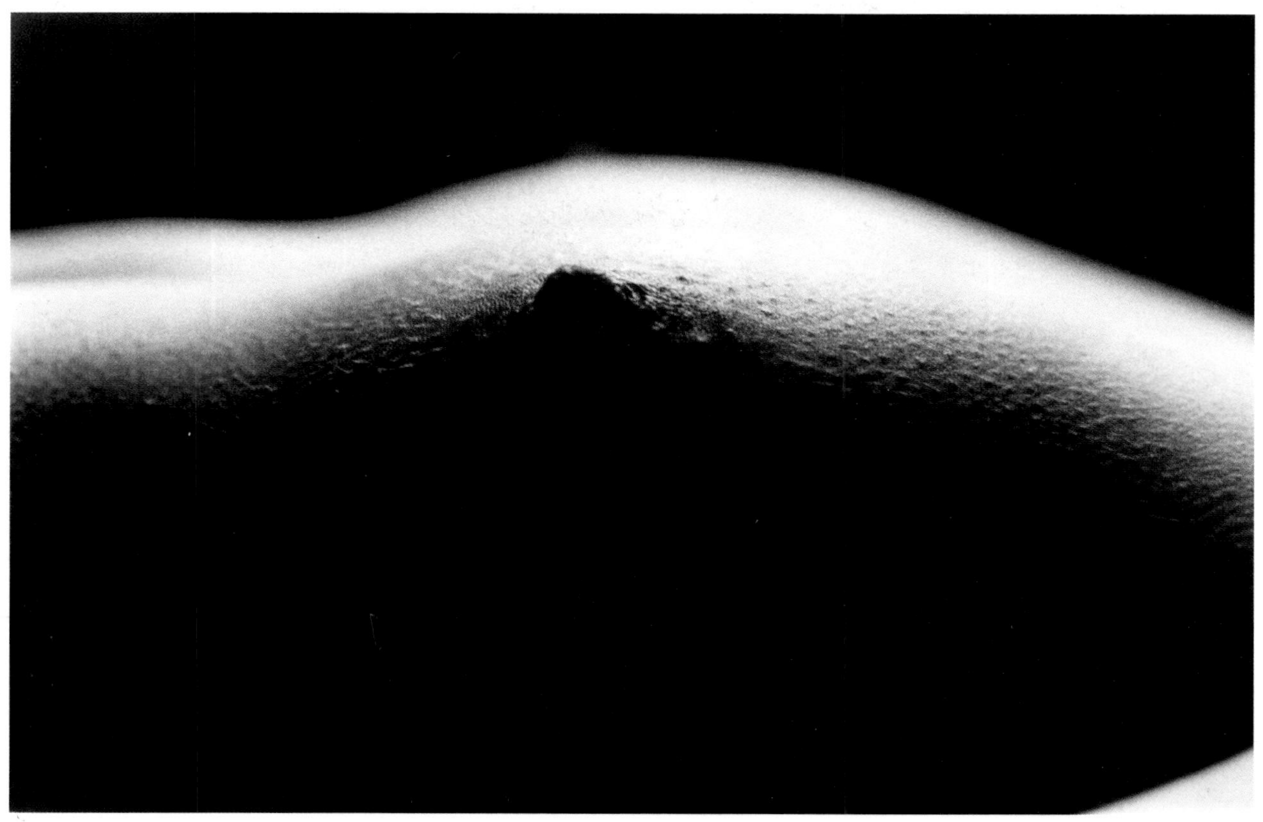

Tim Zika △△
Markus Bollen △

Kimikazu Tomizawa

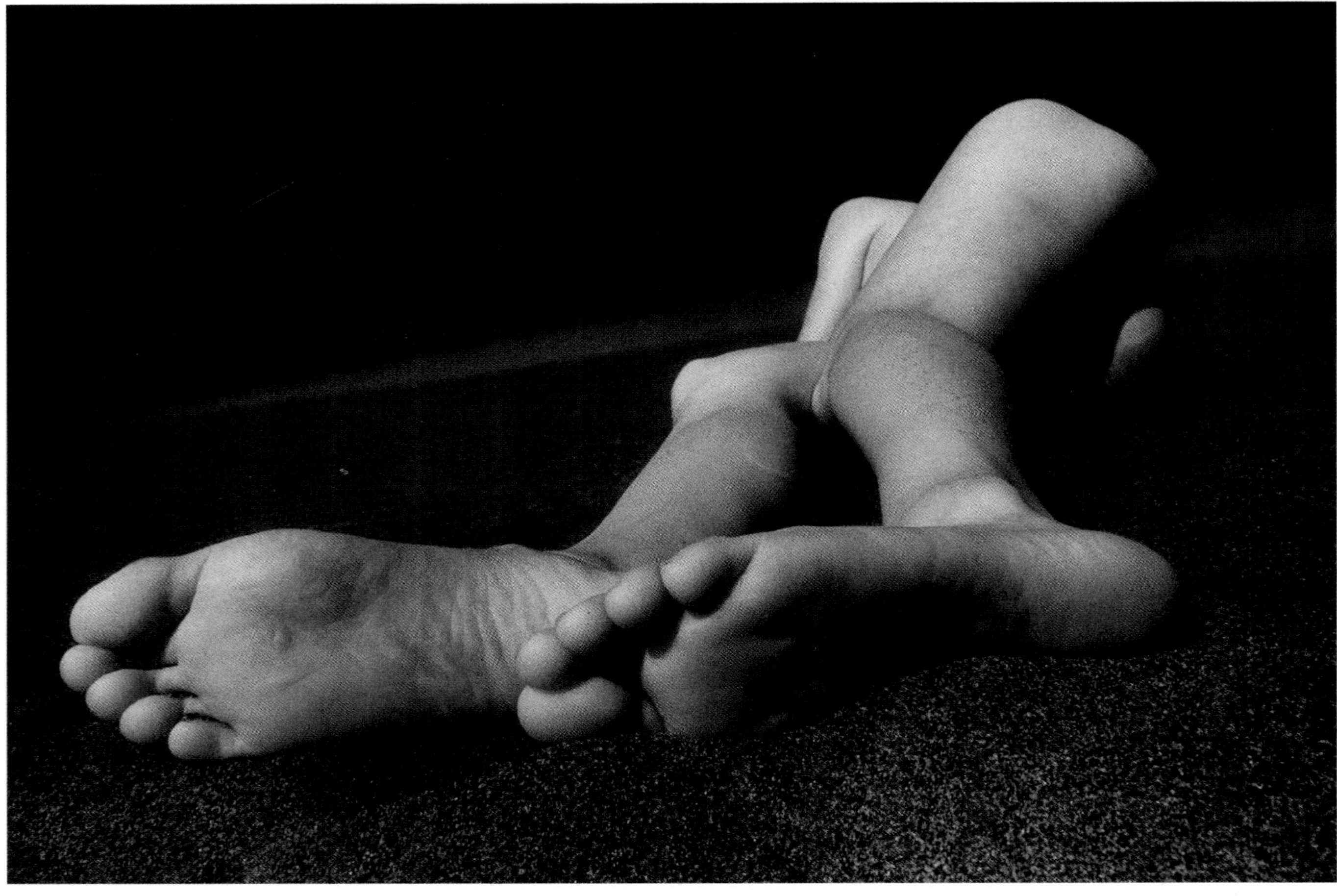

Hisako Sakurai

Frank Rheinboldt

Jürgen Schulzki

Pascal Baetens

Pascal Baetens

George Wieser

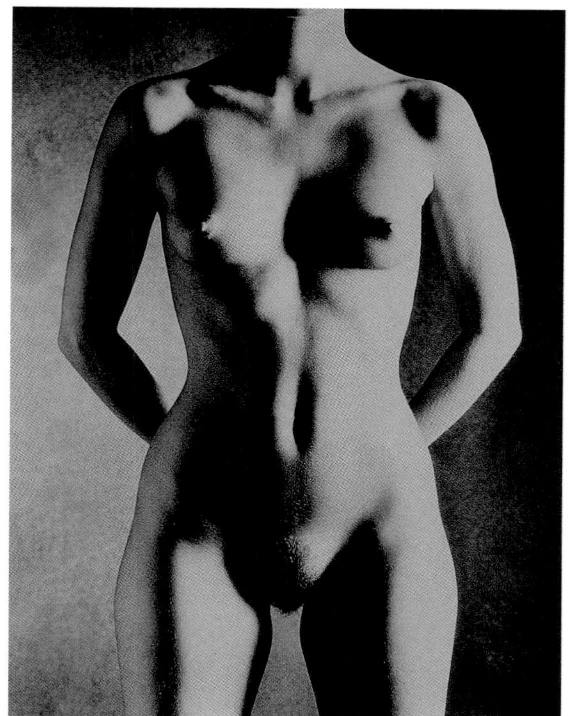

Anne-Marie von Sarosdy

Günter Knop

Patrick Lhullier

Michael Vana

Yuri Dojc

Yuri Dojc

Phil Bekker

Mike Horseman

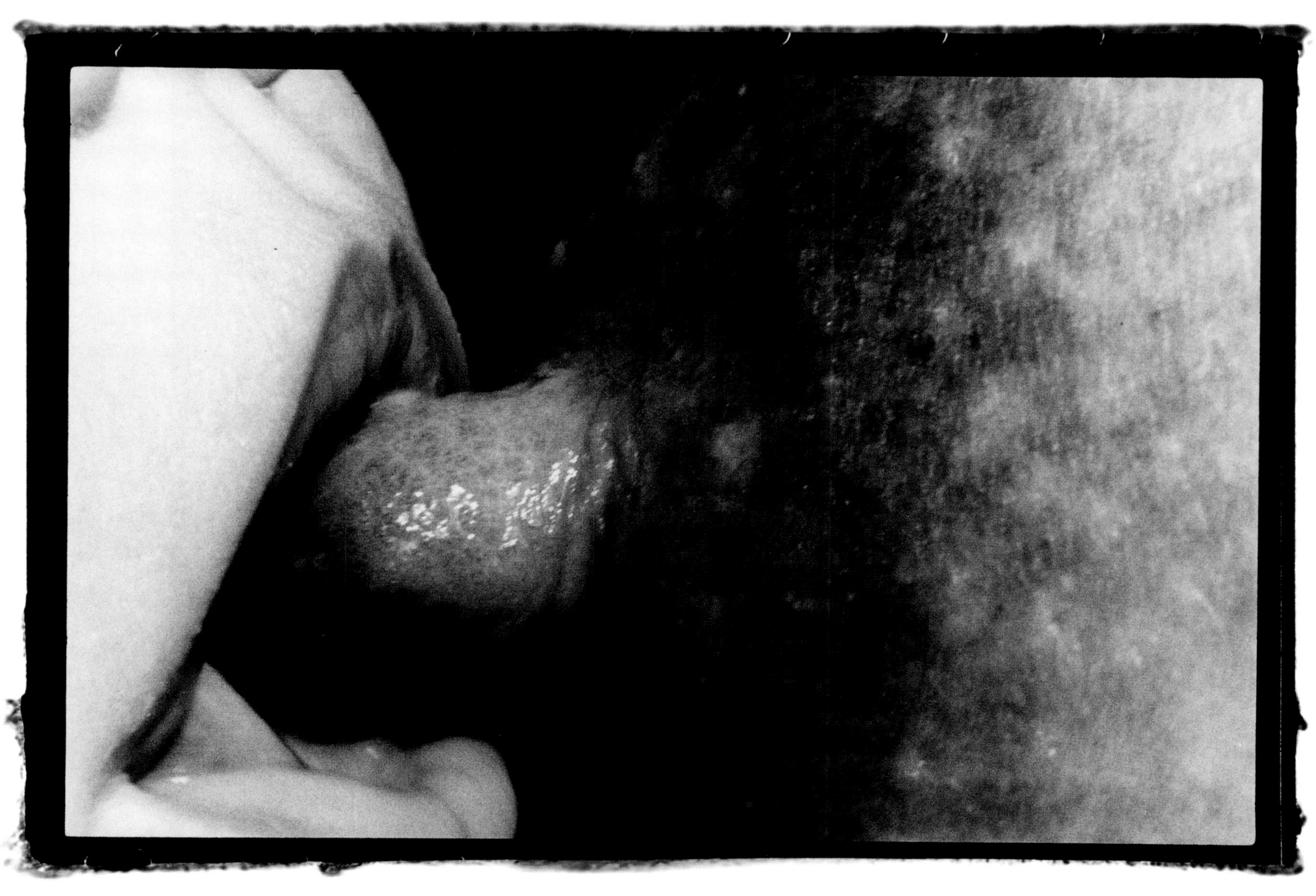

Archie Kent

Thomas Schlömann

Wolfgang Eichler

Claude Fauville

Sergio Assabbi

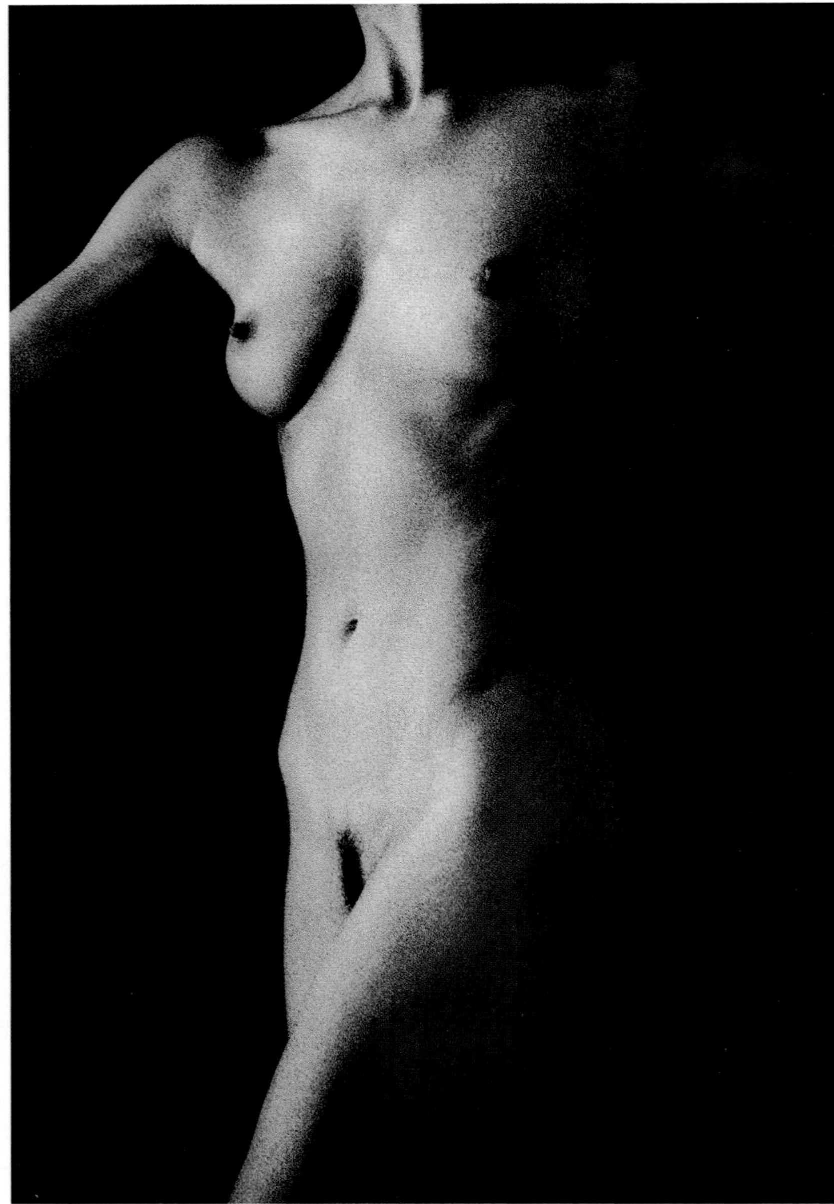

Richard Bradbury

Brigitte Tast

Xavier Bonnin

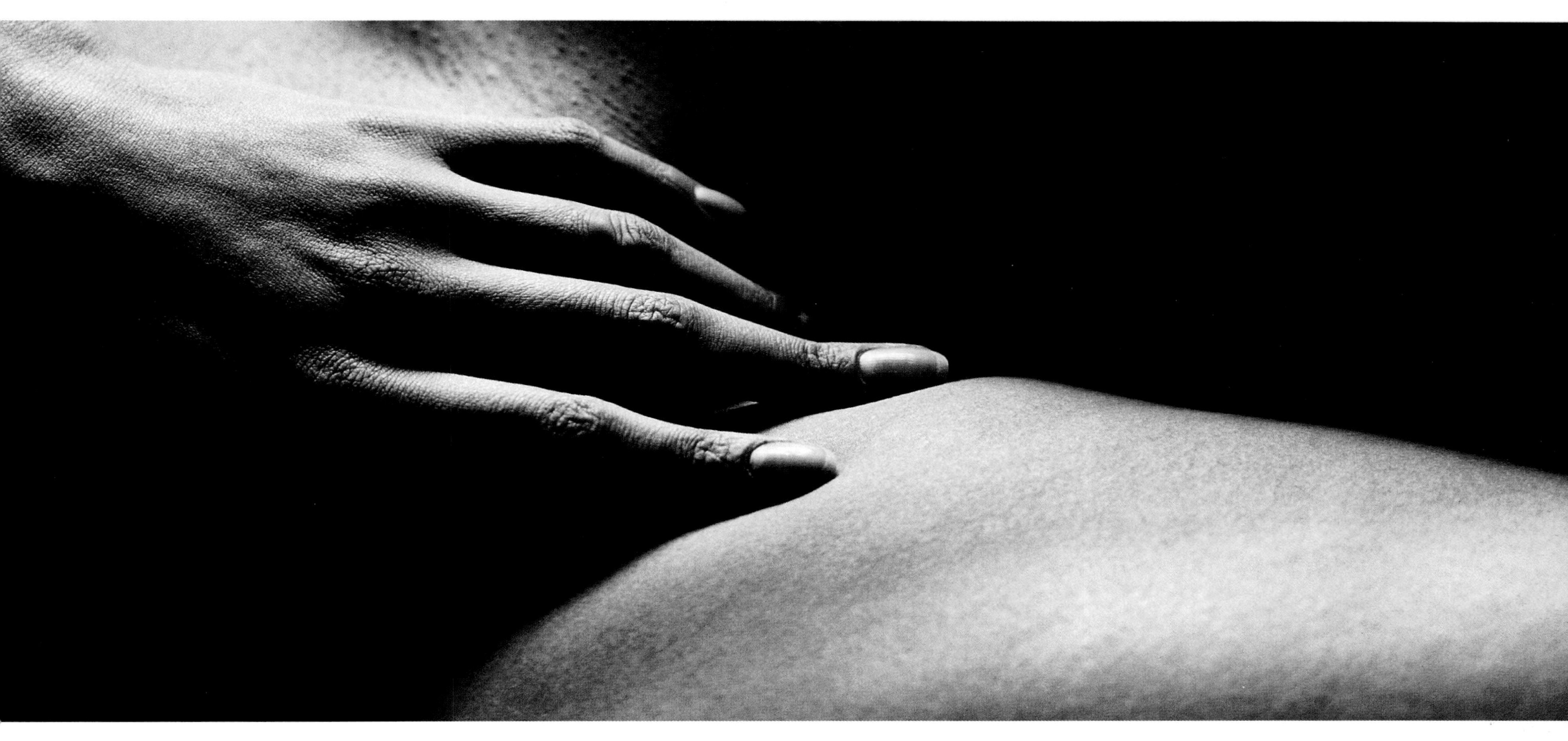

Xavier Bonnin

Ralph Weber

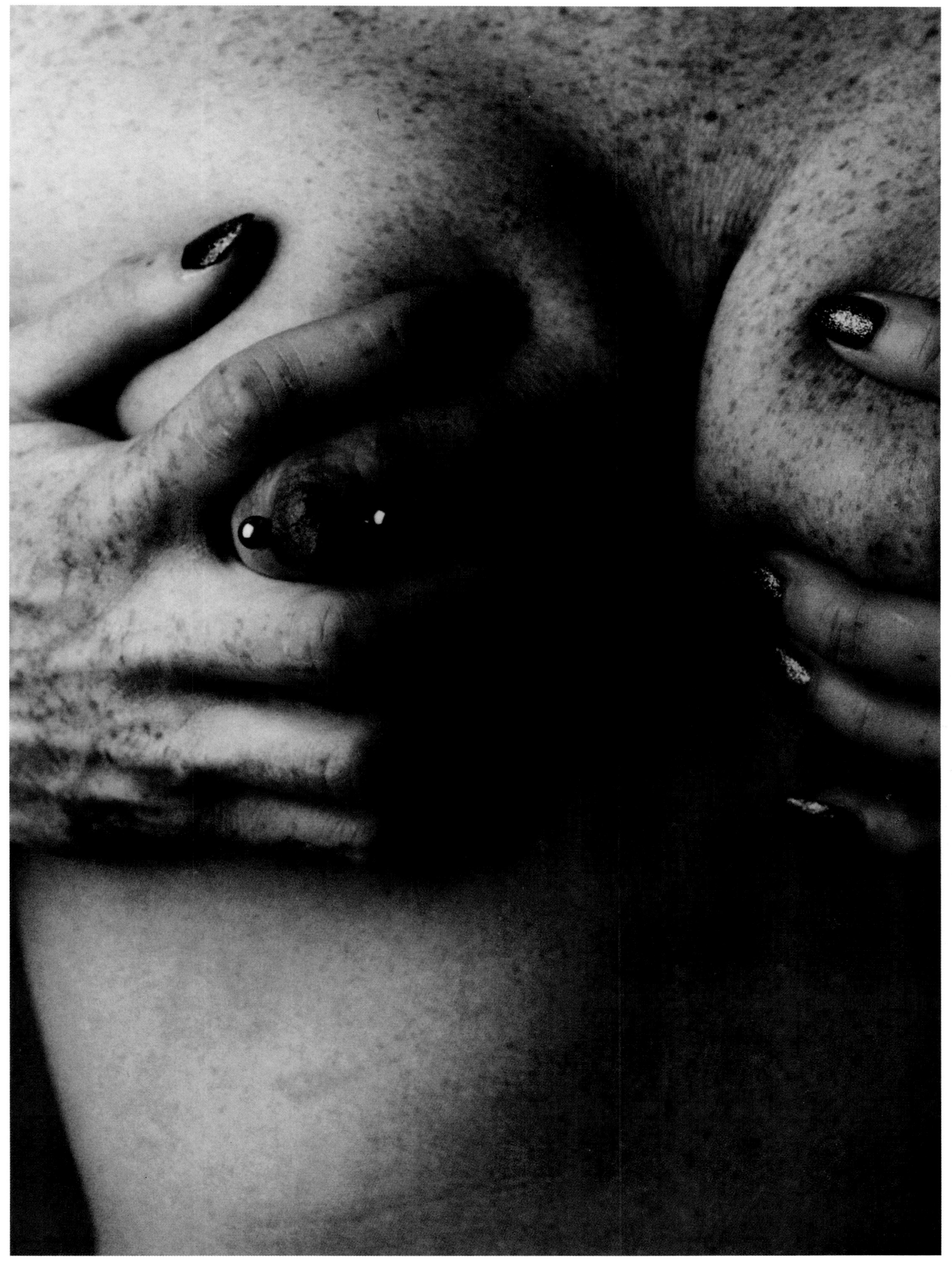

Jan Tepass

Peter Dazeley

Torsten Andreas Hoffmann

Melk Imboden

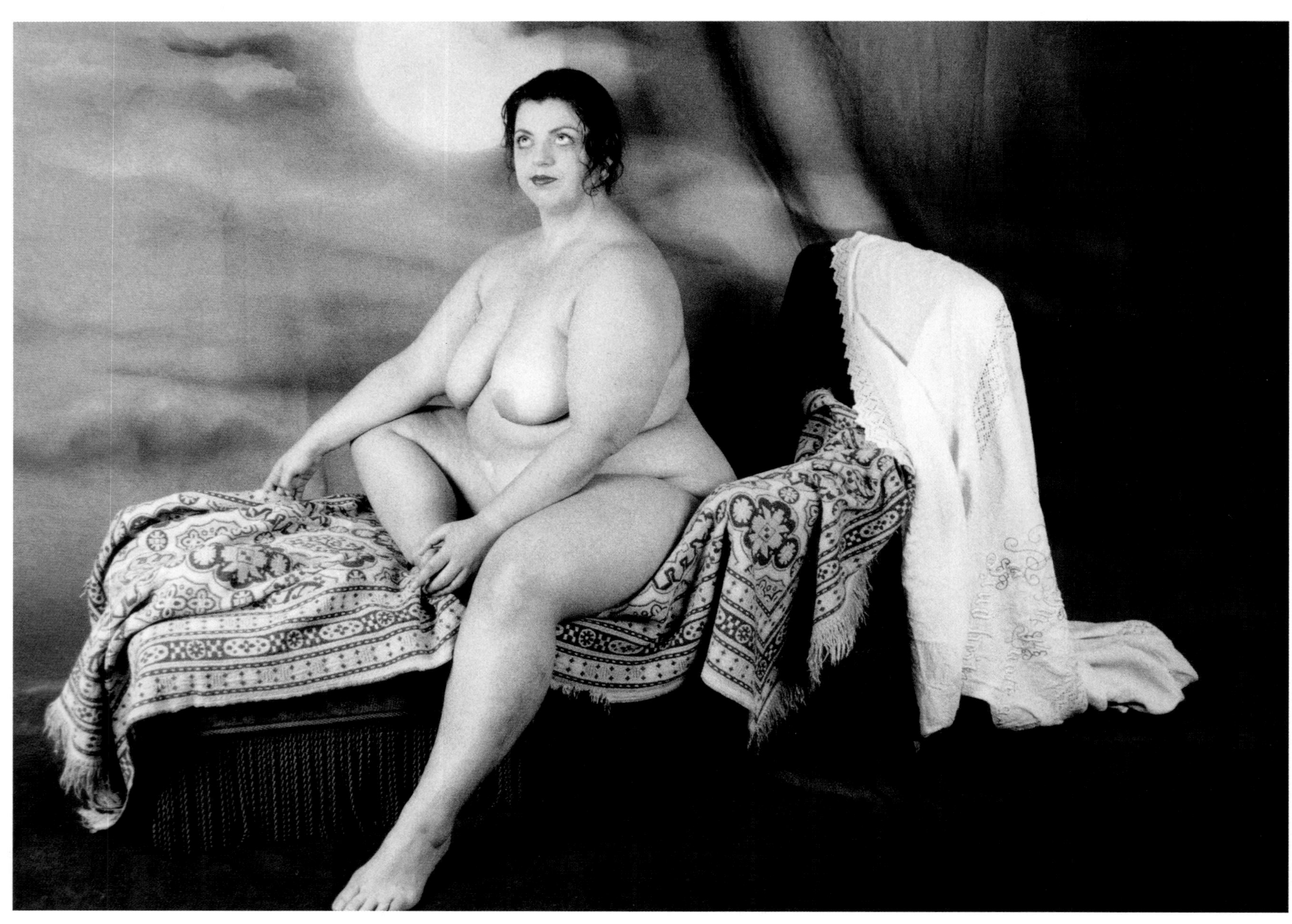

Hildegard M. Wilms

Catherine Steinmann

Nick Dolding

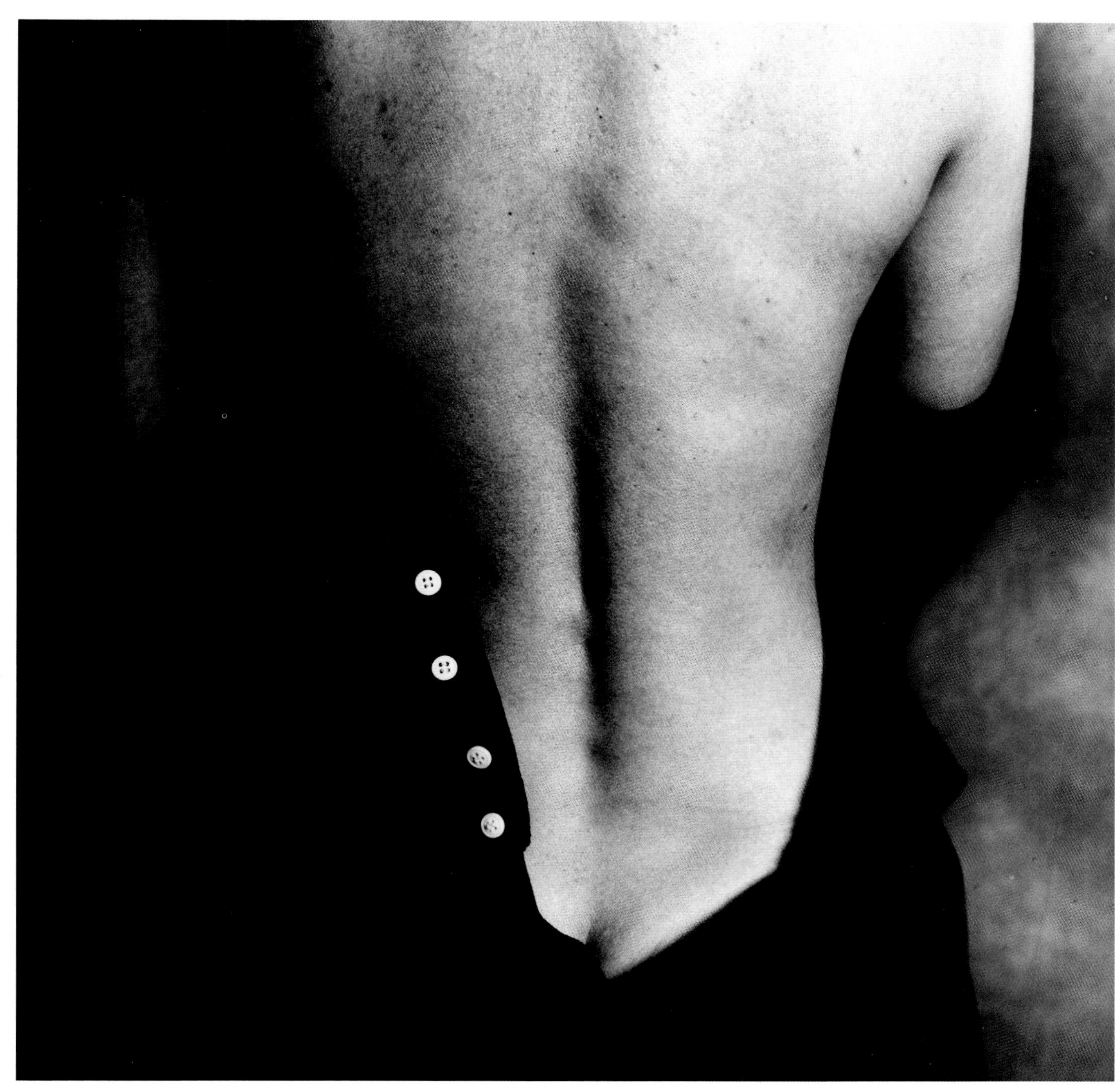

Marcelo Isarrualde

Pascale Jansen

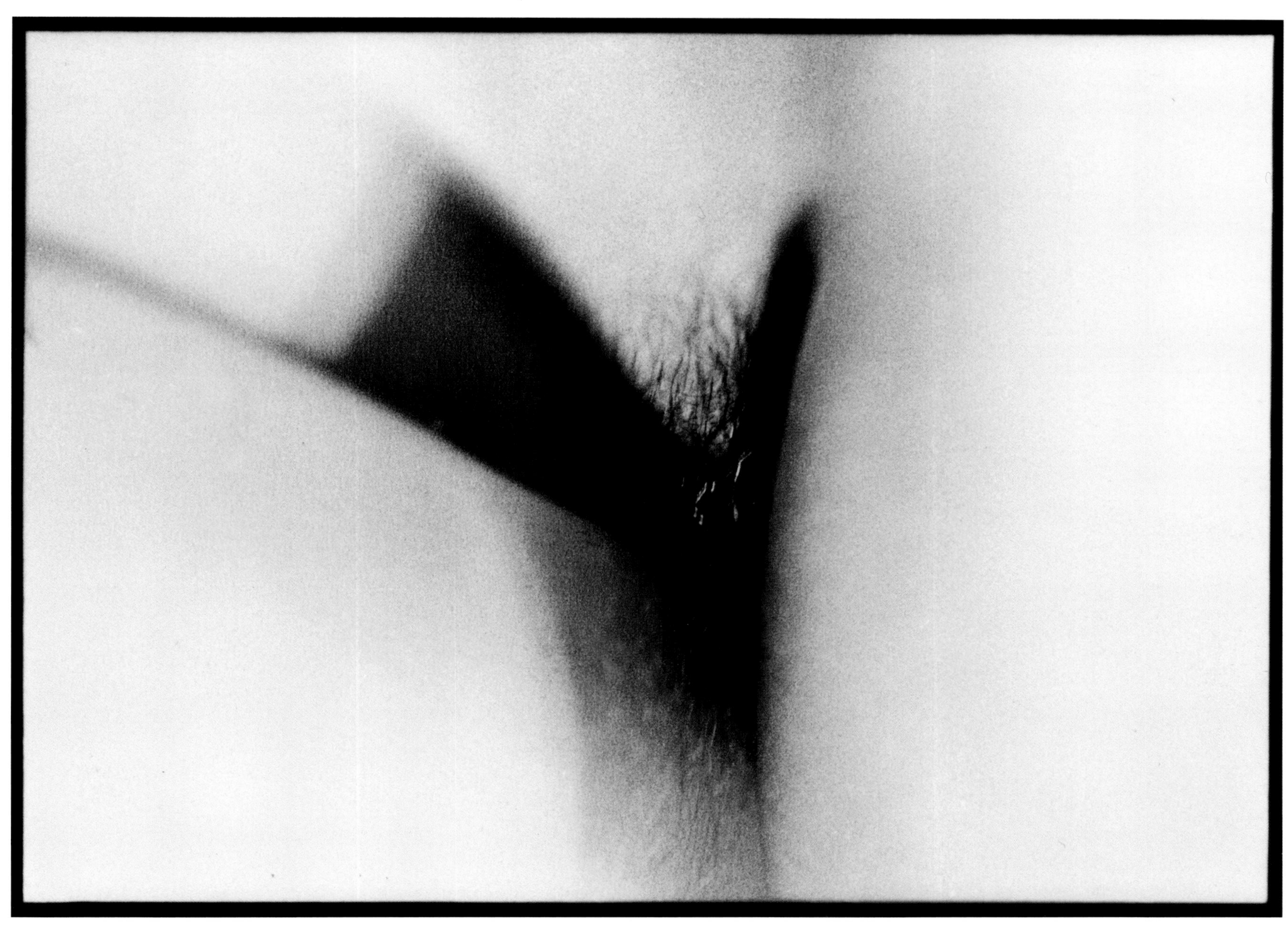

Alexander Döring

Uwe Kempen

Michael Vana

Gerhard Vormwald

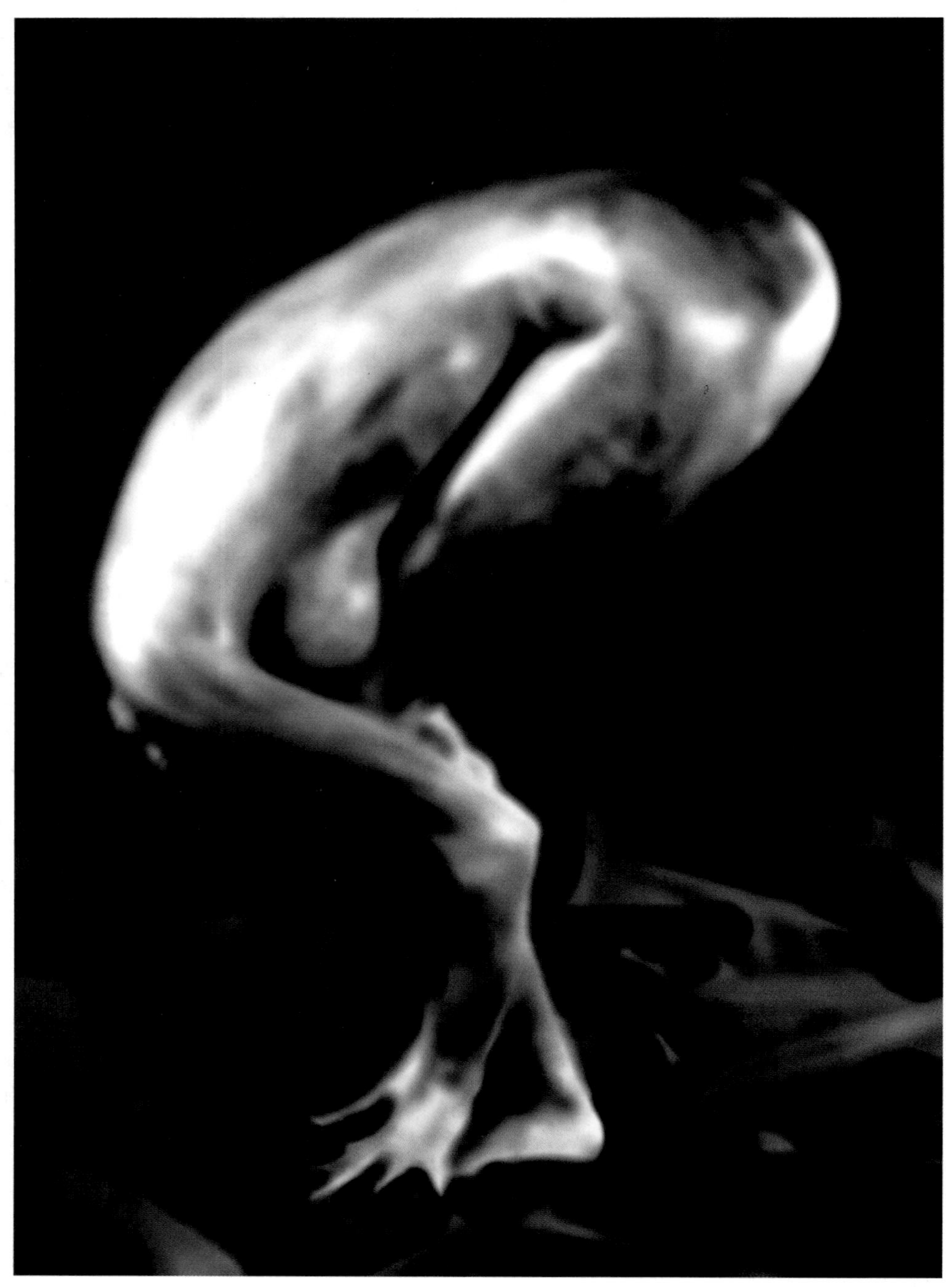

Irmgard Elsner

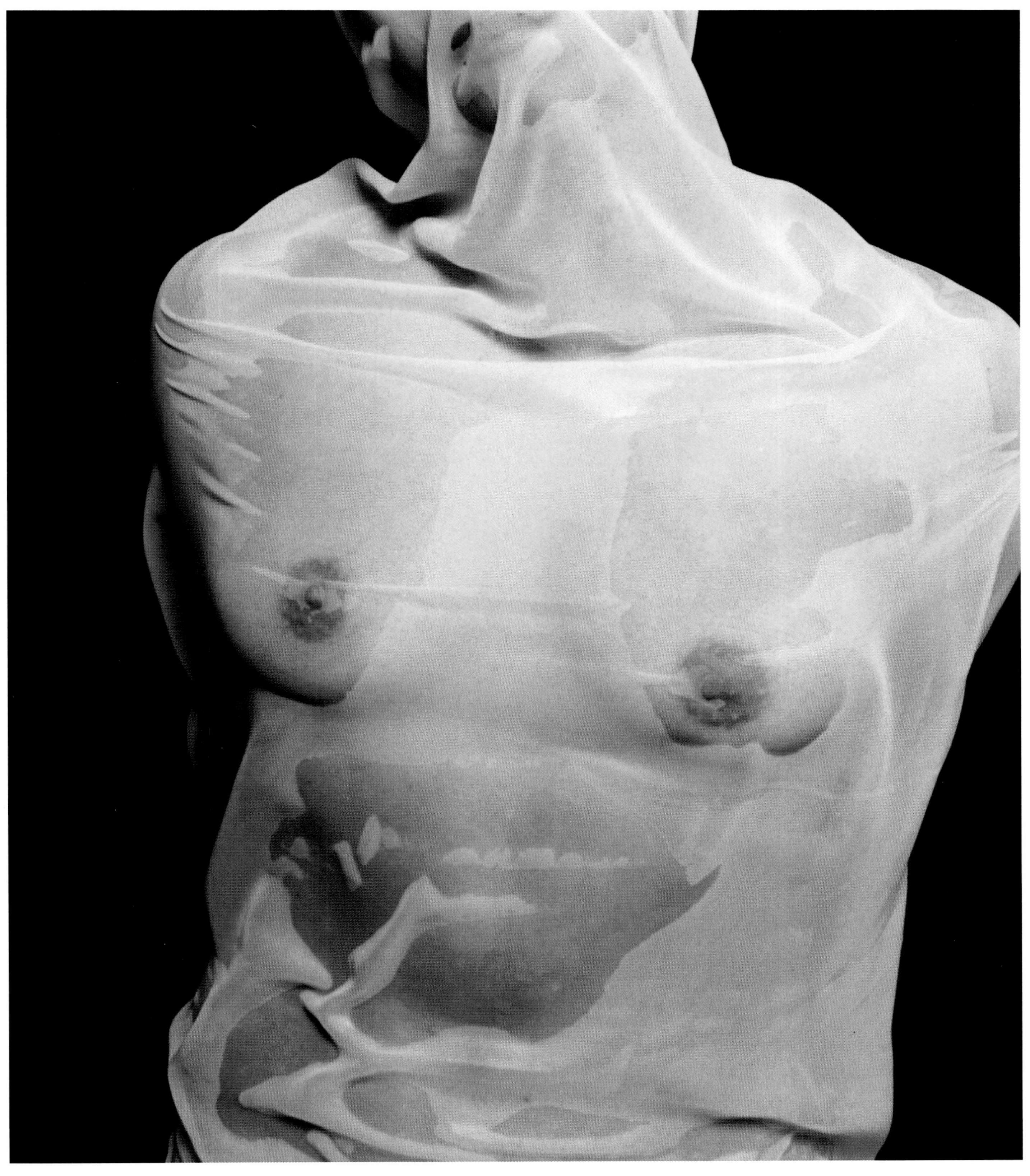

Patrick Naughton

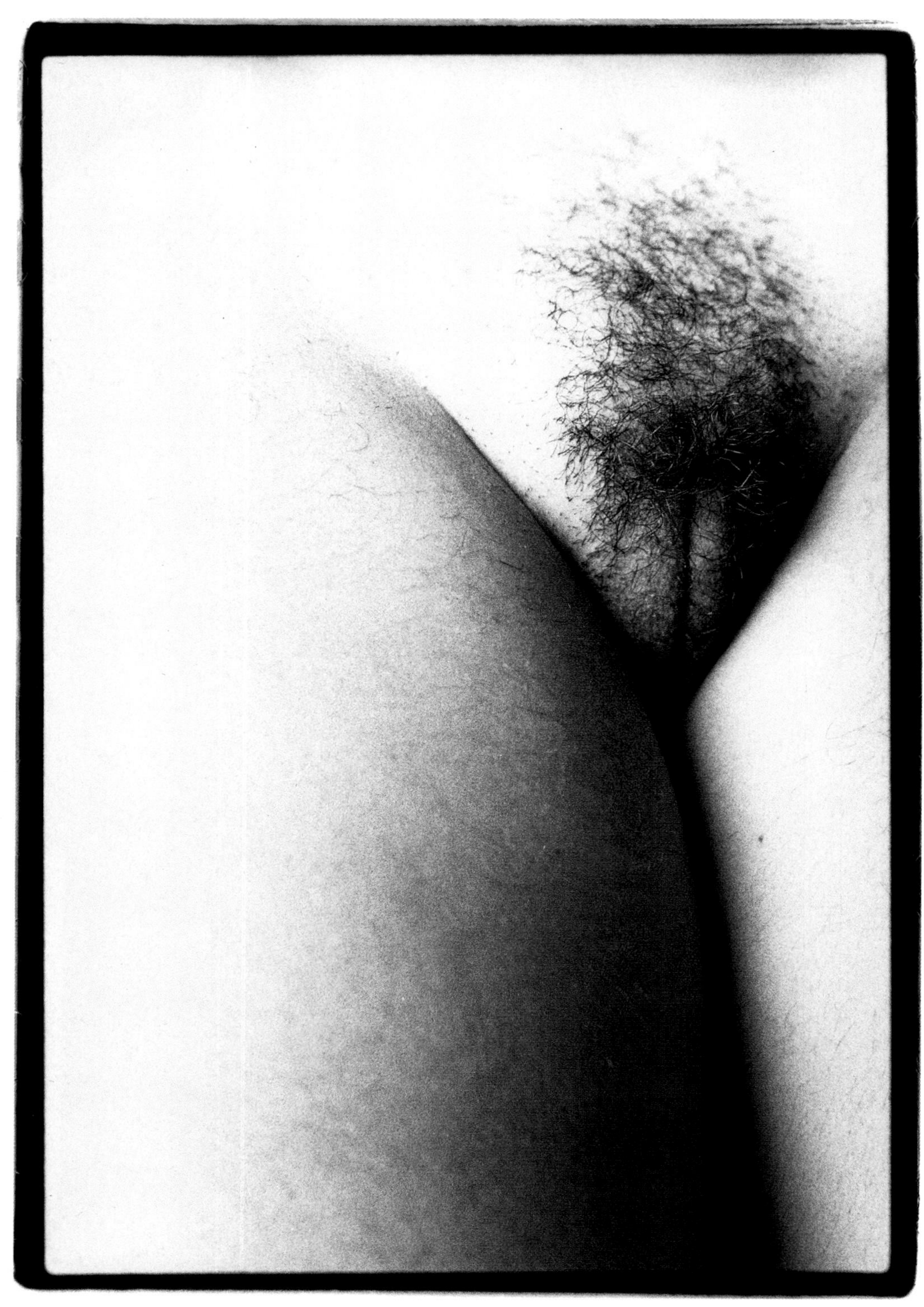

Graham Monro

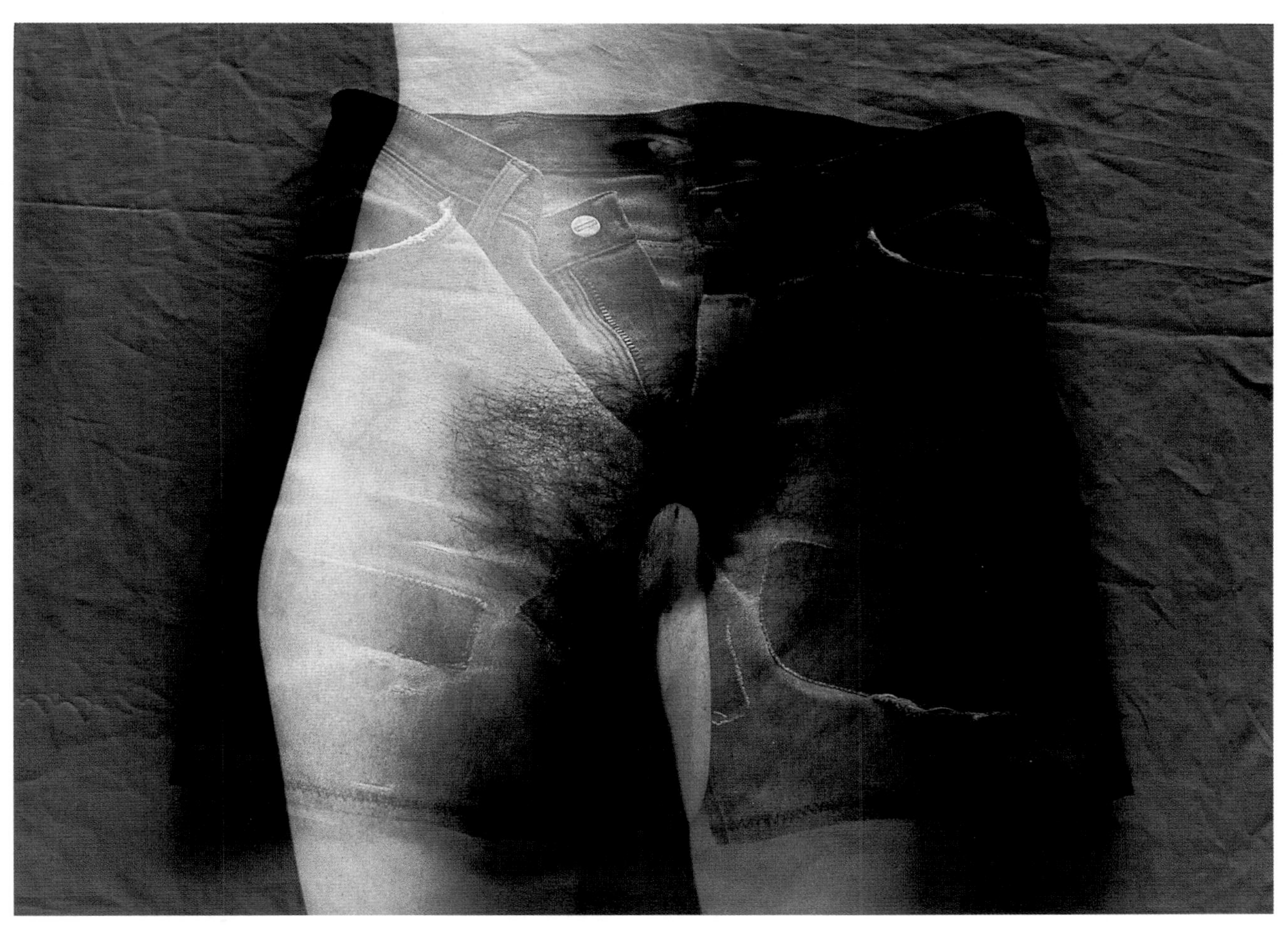

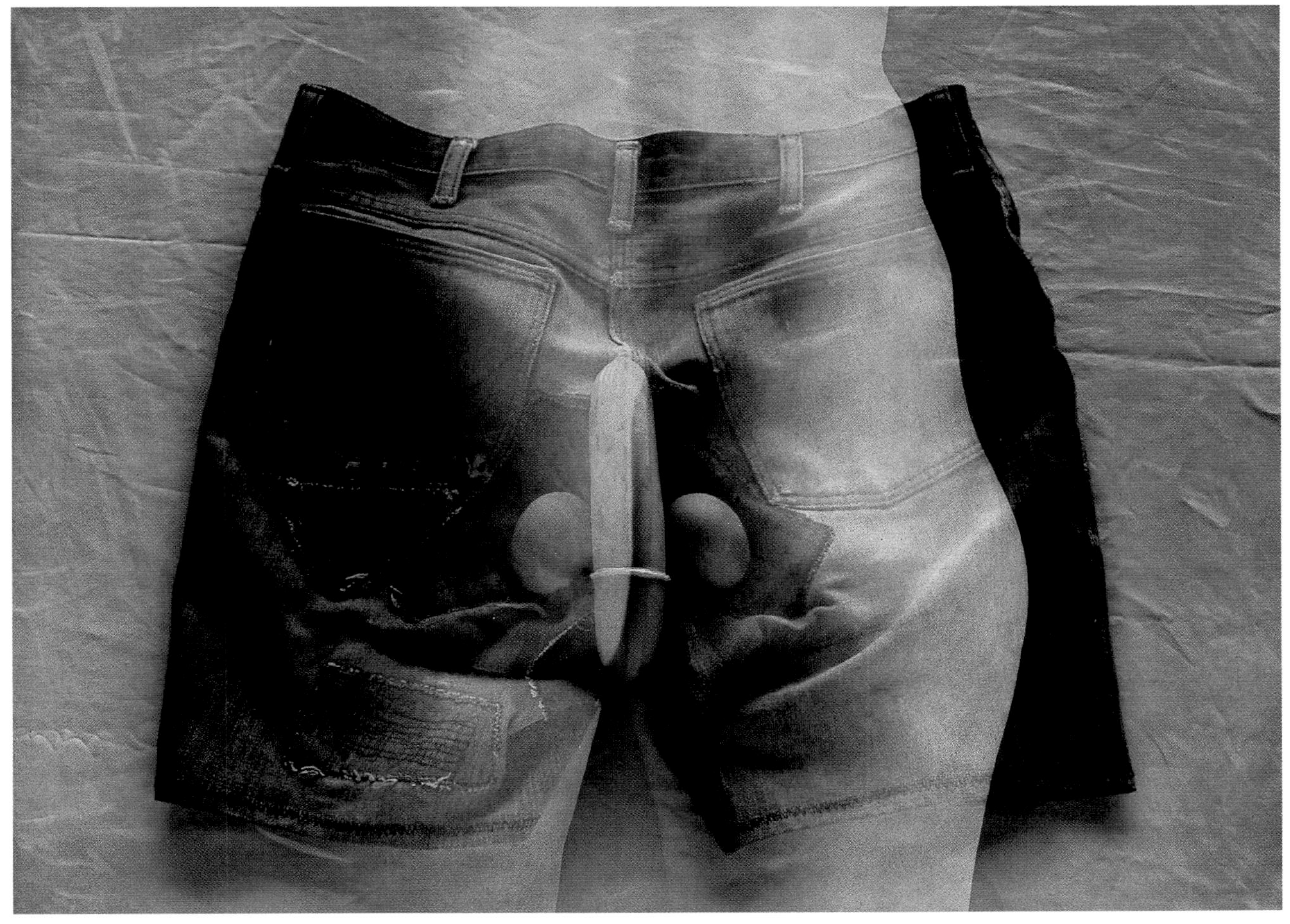

Vadim Filimonov

Lynn Goldsmith

Alva Bernadine

Abe Frajndlich

Manfred Wirtz

MALE I

Vesselin Valtchev

◂ ◂ Jörn Hartmann

Garrie Maguire

Heinz Henschel ▷

Joao Fernando Romao Dias da Silva

E. R. Malmström

Renata Ratajczyk

Almond Chu

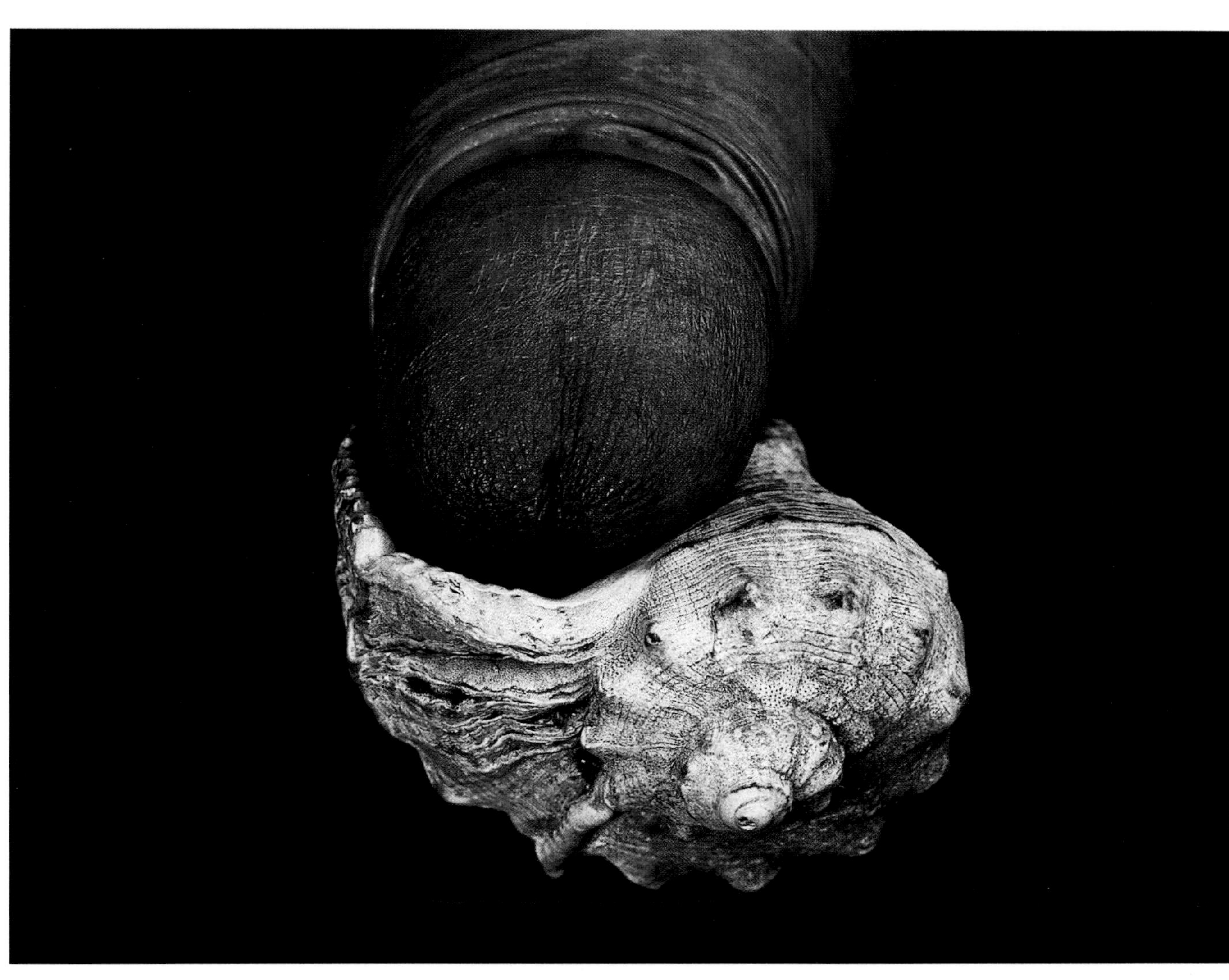

Vadim Filimonov

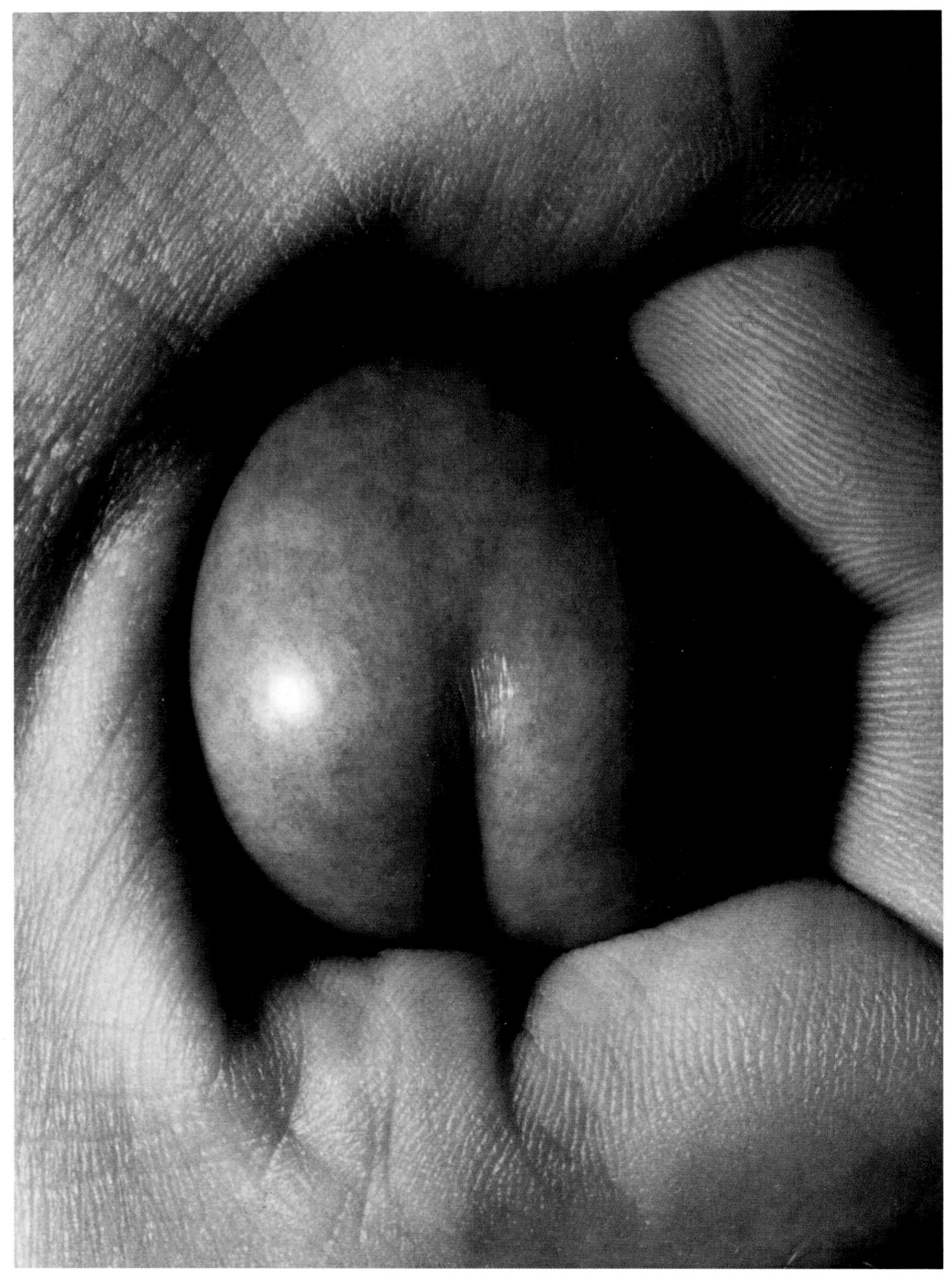

Jan Tepass

Almond Chu

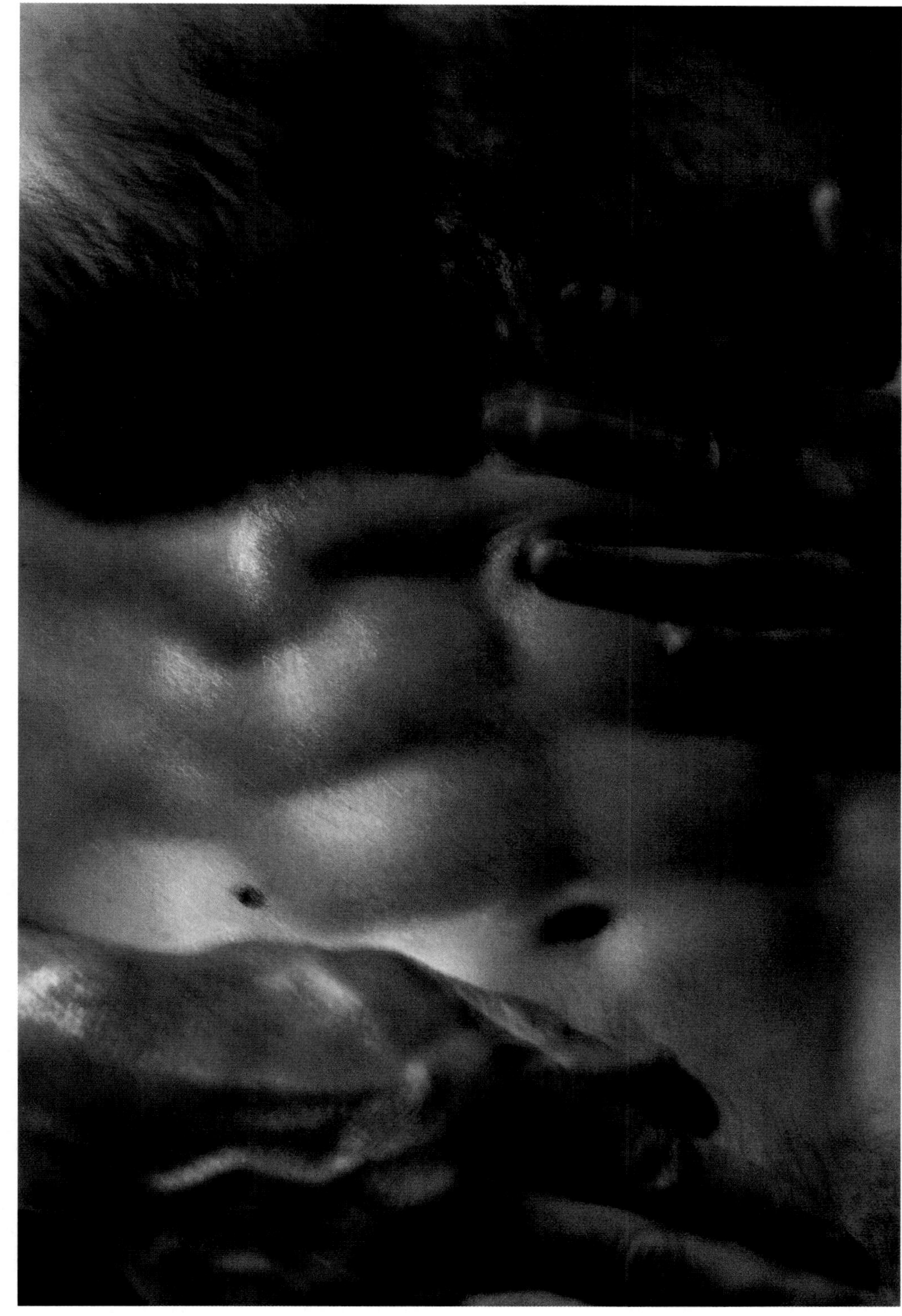

Tim Zika

◁ Benno Thoma

Anderson & Low

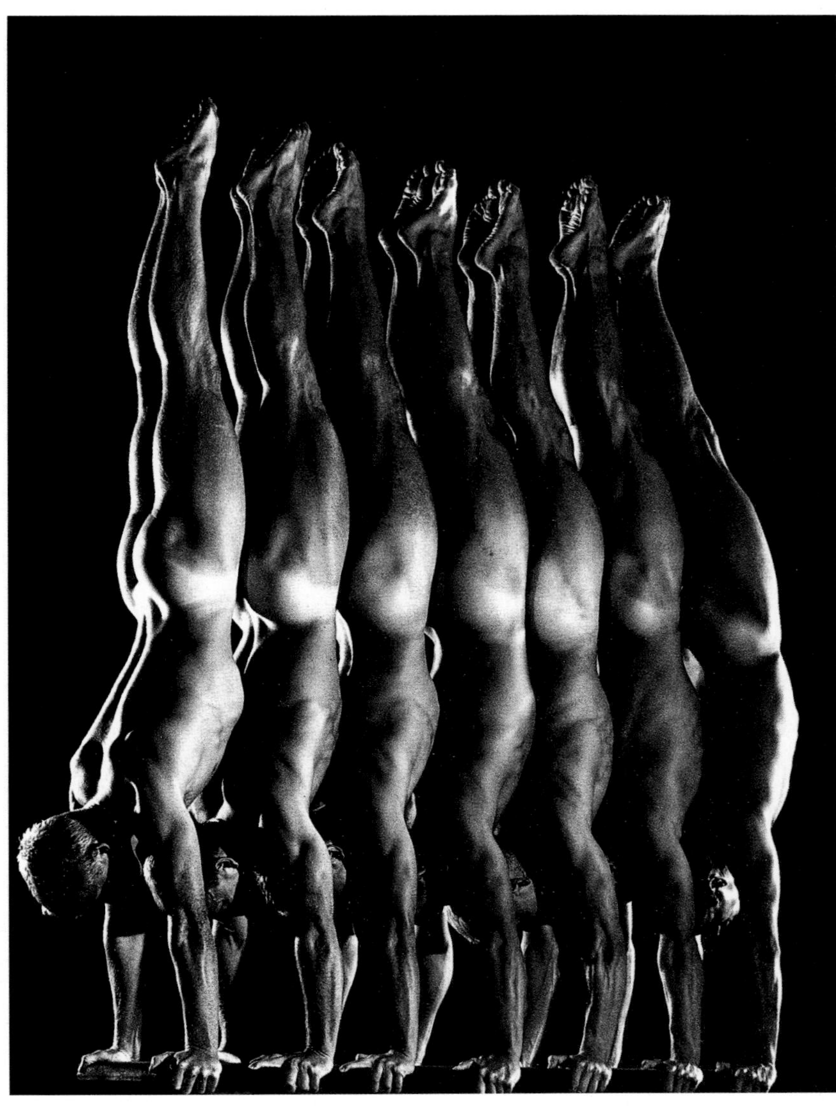

Anderson & Low

◁ Heinz Henschel

Ed Freeman

Ed Freeman

Frank Rheinboldt

Anne-Marie von Sarosdy

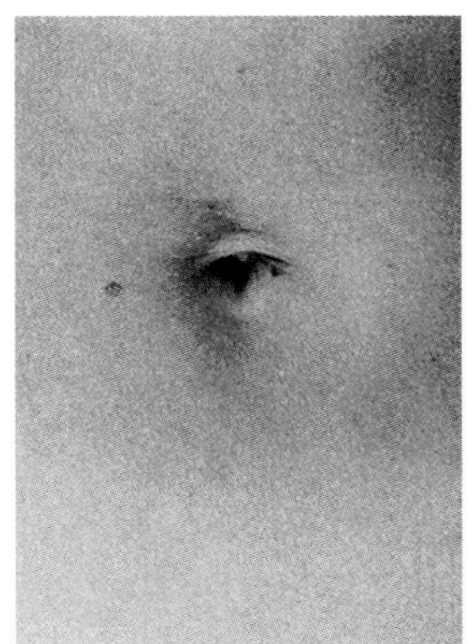

Regina Recht

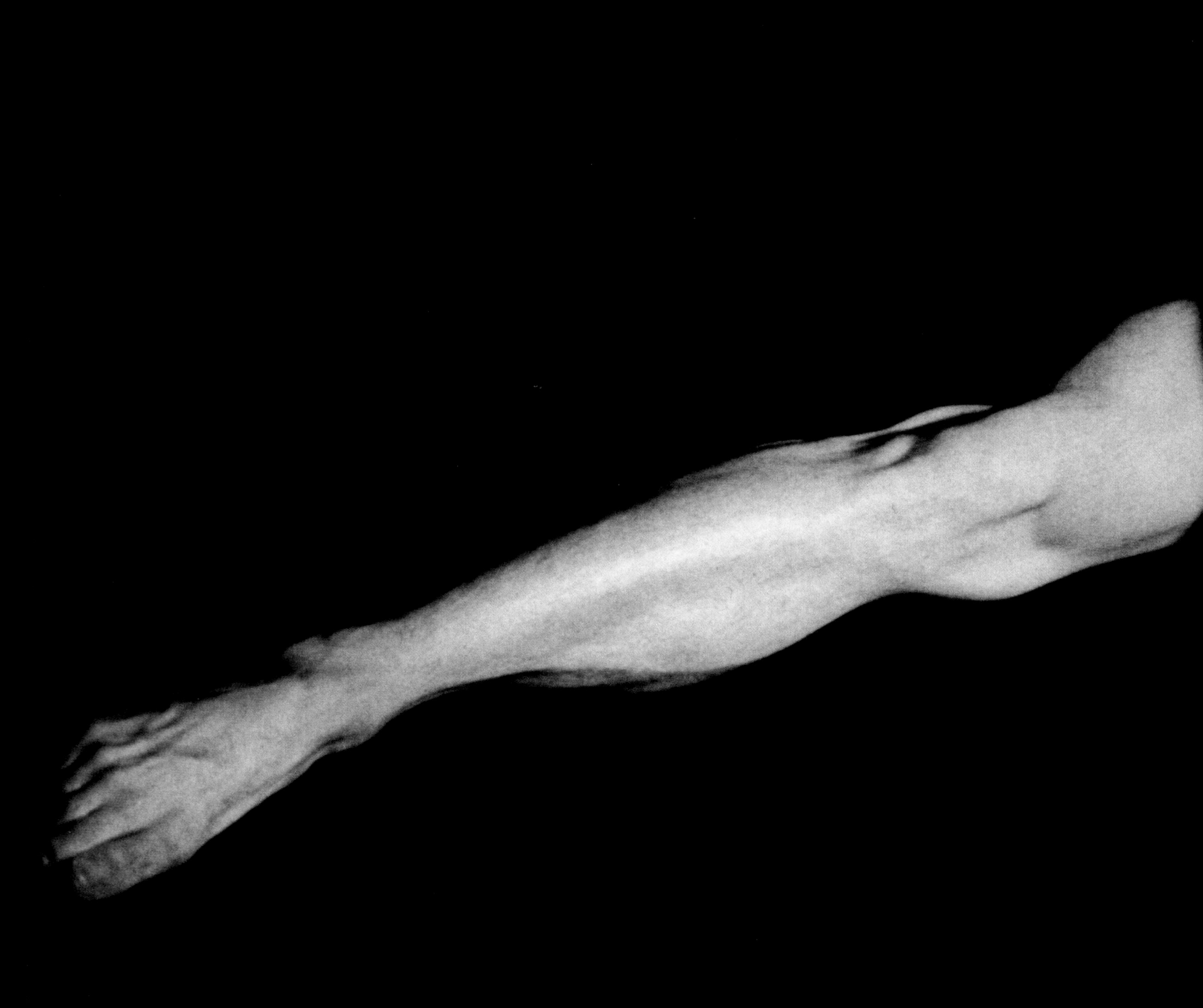

Barbara Traub

◂◂ Günter Knop

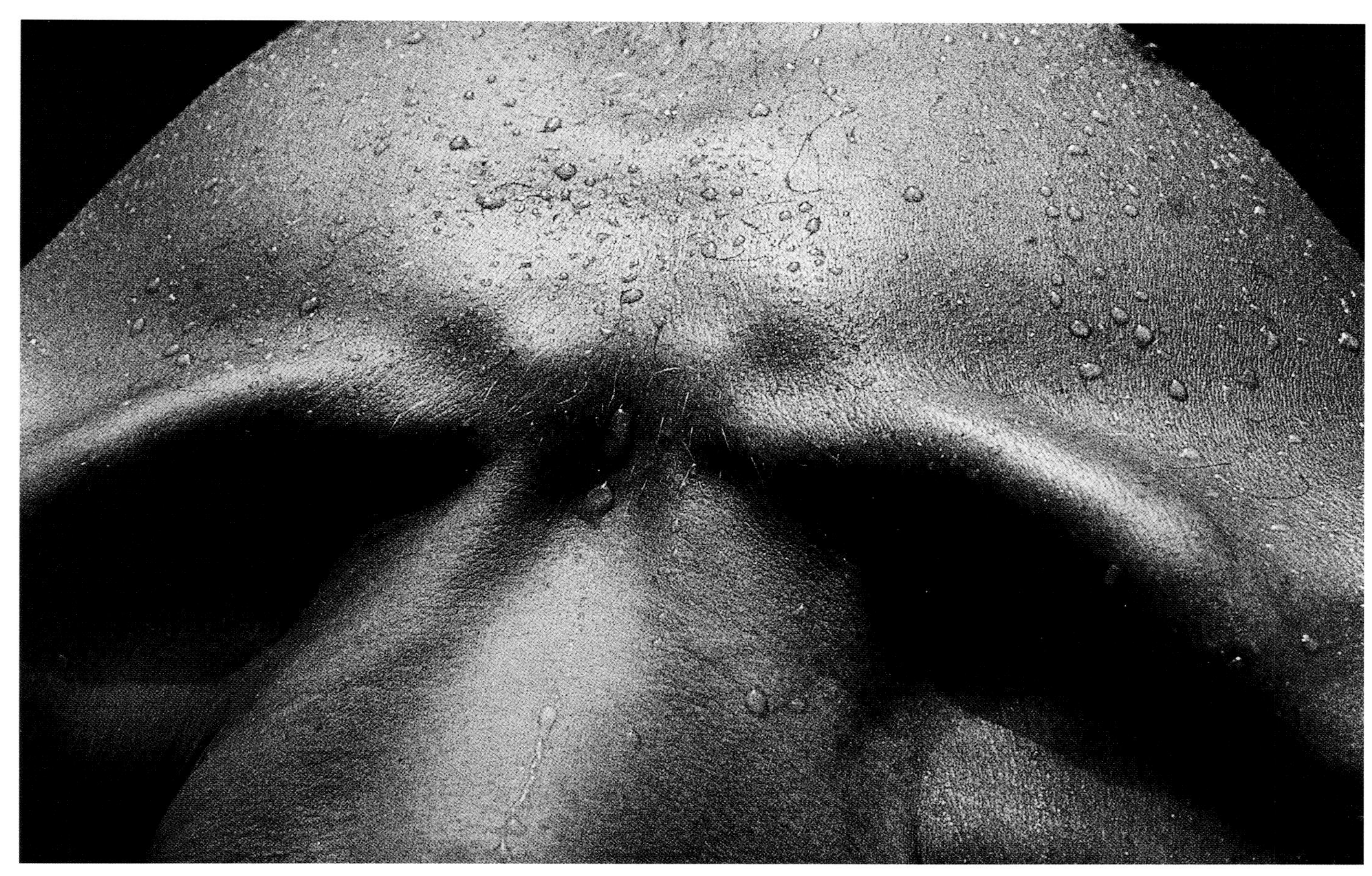

Barbara Traub

Michael Dannenmann

◁ E. R. Malmström

Elisabeth Wiesner

Jörn Hartmann

Michael Bidner

Garrie Maguire

Benno Thoma

Ann Brown

COUPLES

◂◂ Anne-Marie von Sarosdy △

Archie Kent

Dietrich Halemeyer

Dan Nelken

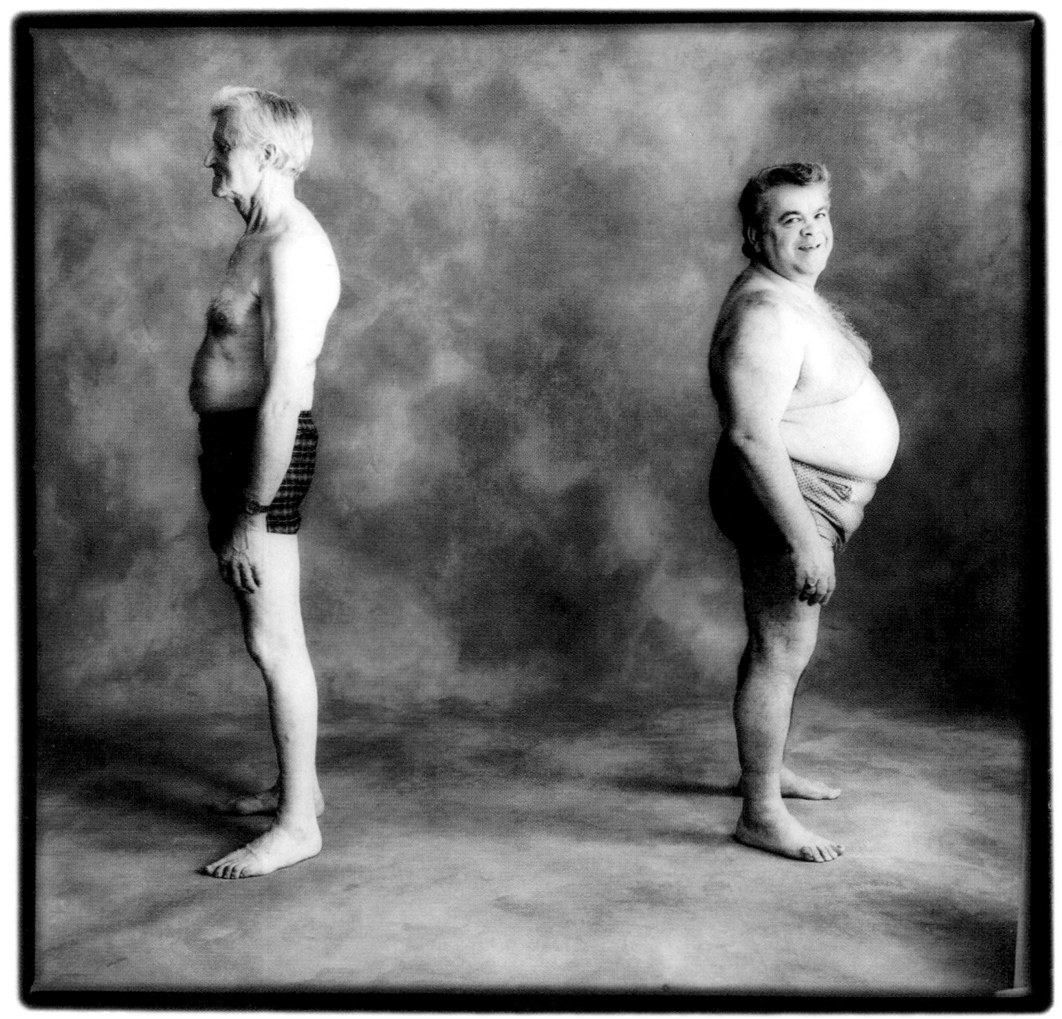

Alfons Iseli

Dietrich Halemeyer

Onofre Bachiller

Onofre Bachiller

Sinje Dillenkofer

Patrick Naughton

◁ Anne-Marie von Sarosdy

Ansgar Pudenz/Rusch

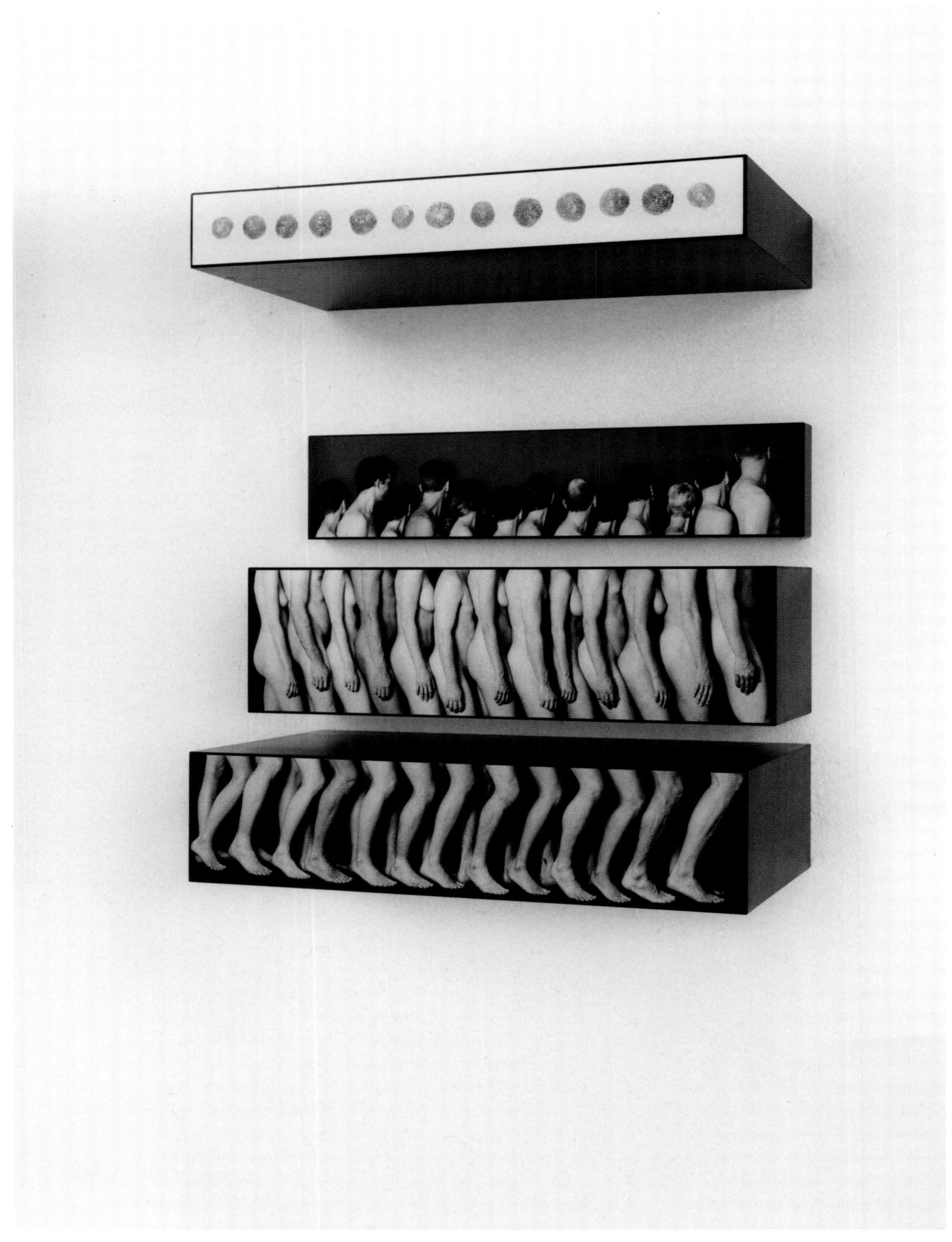

Sinje Dillenkofer

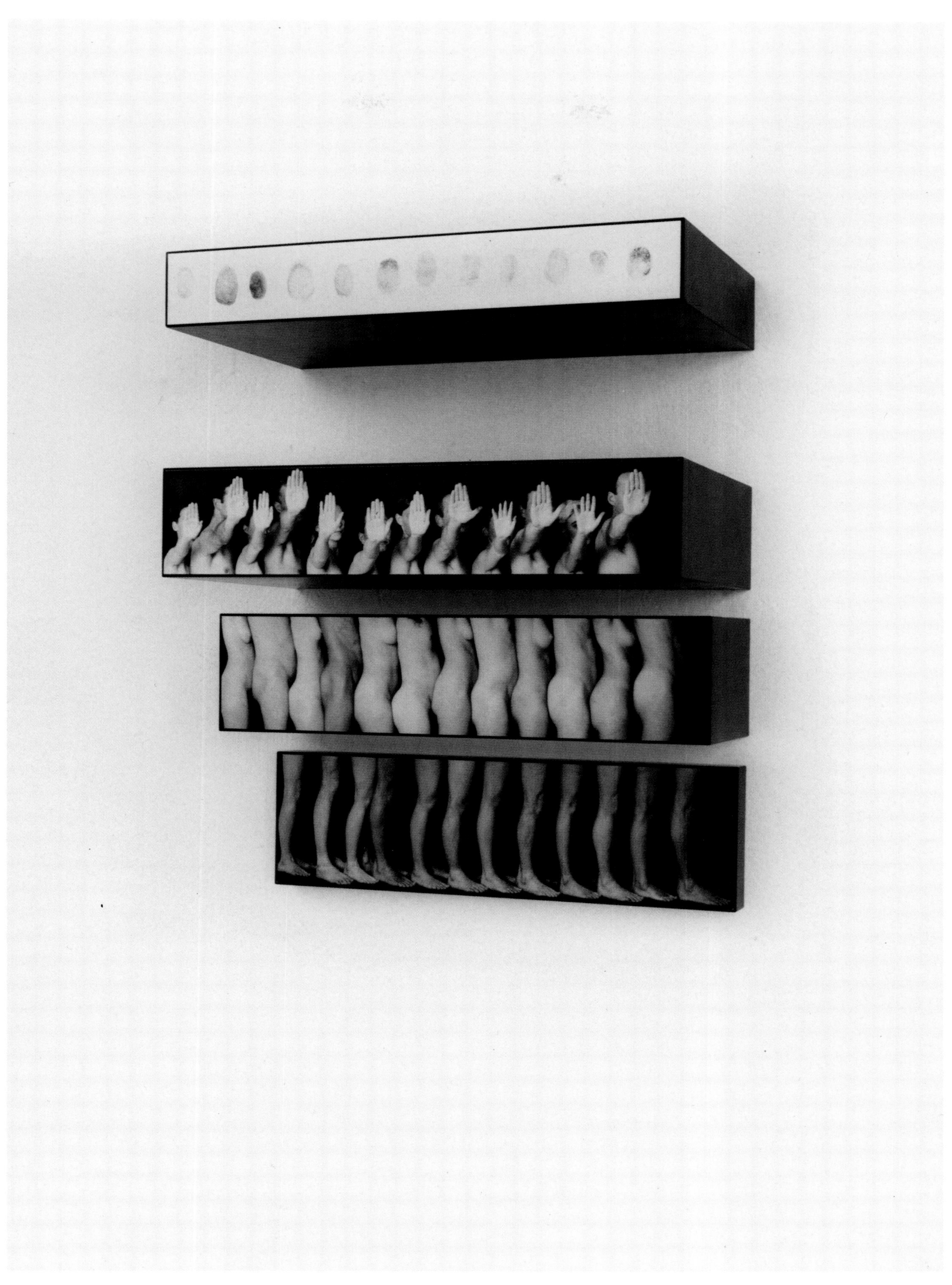

Christoph Büschel

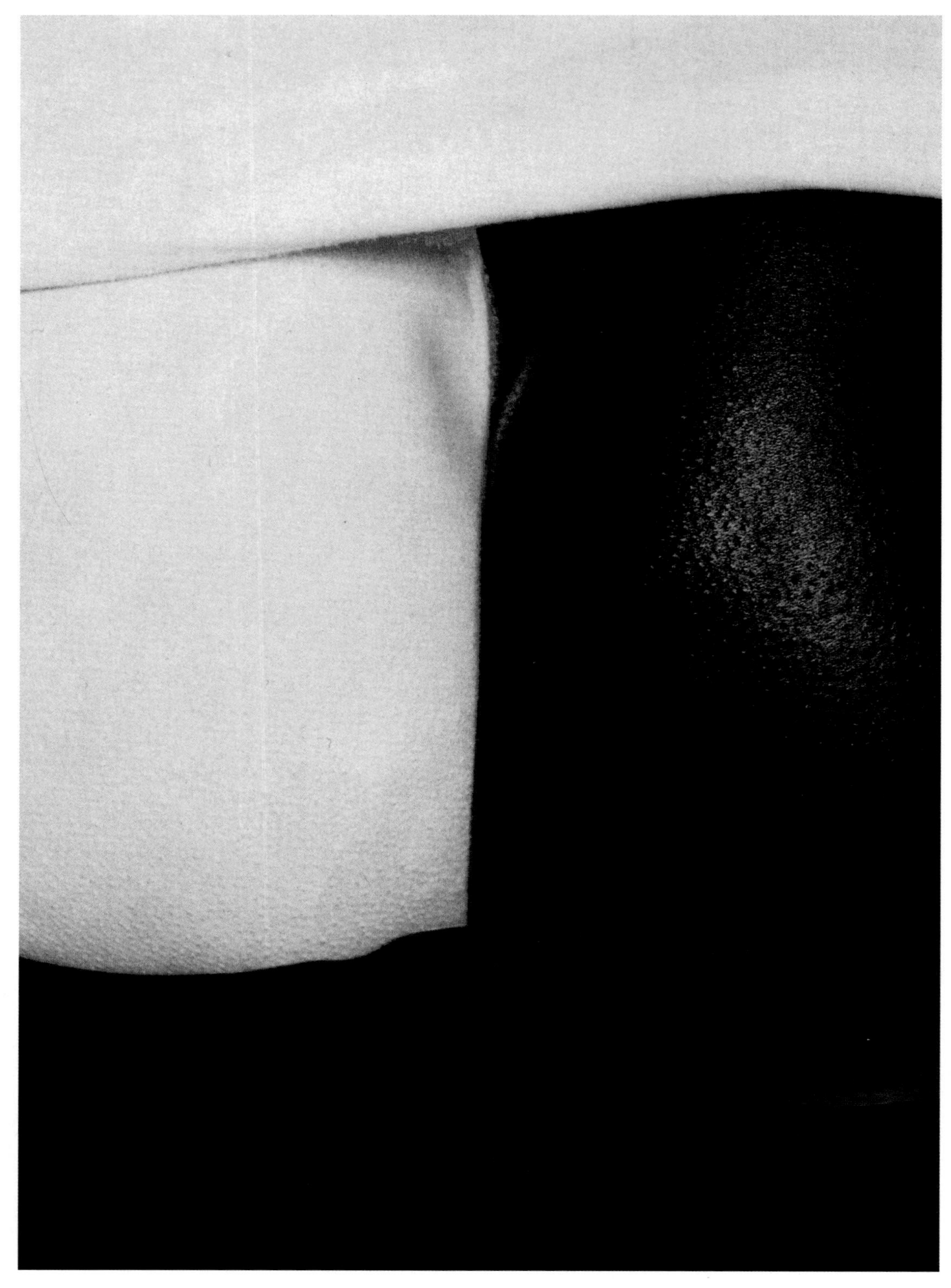

Peter Adler

Michael E. Northrup

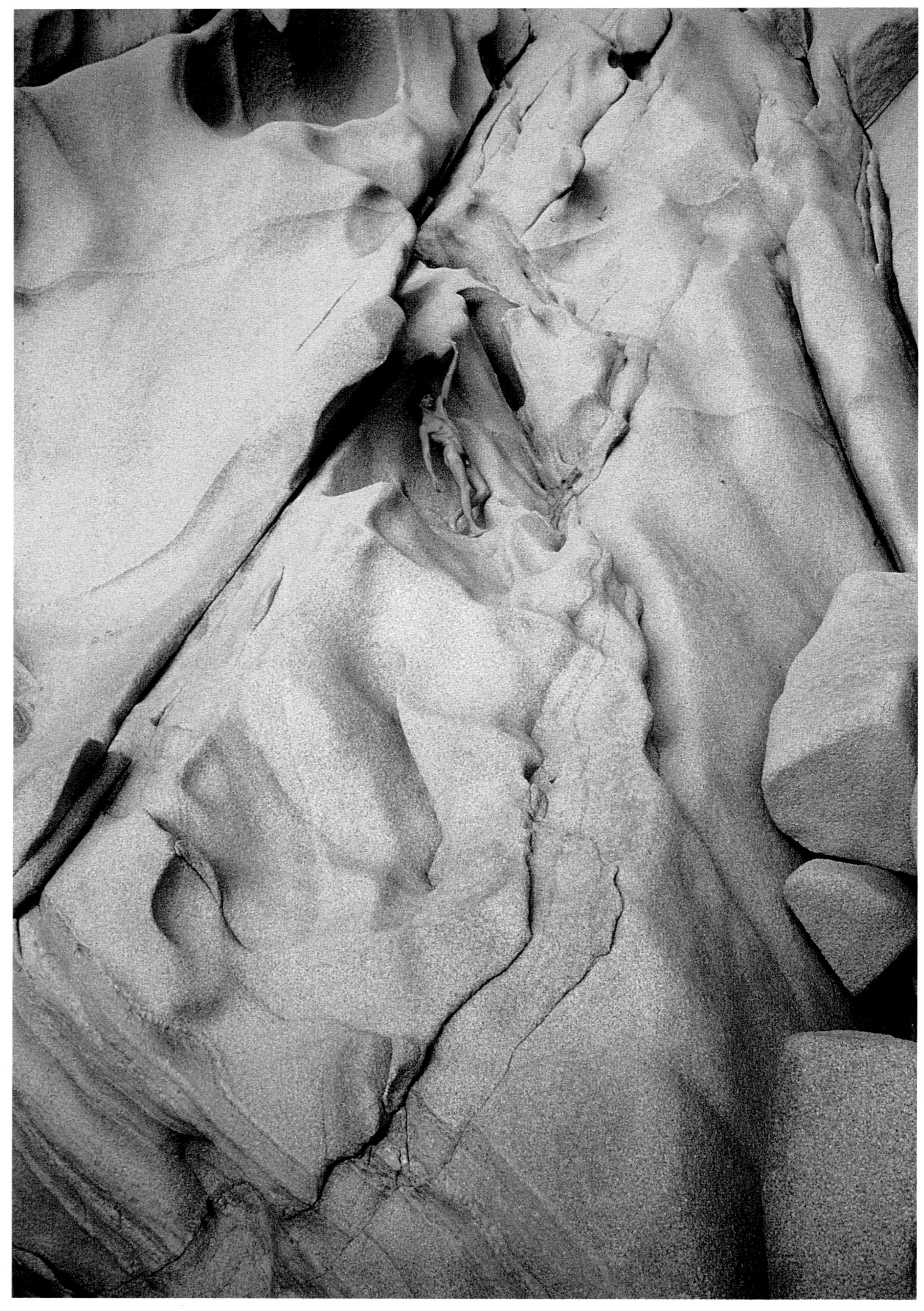

Zefiro & Luna

Zefiro & Luna

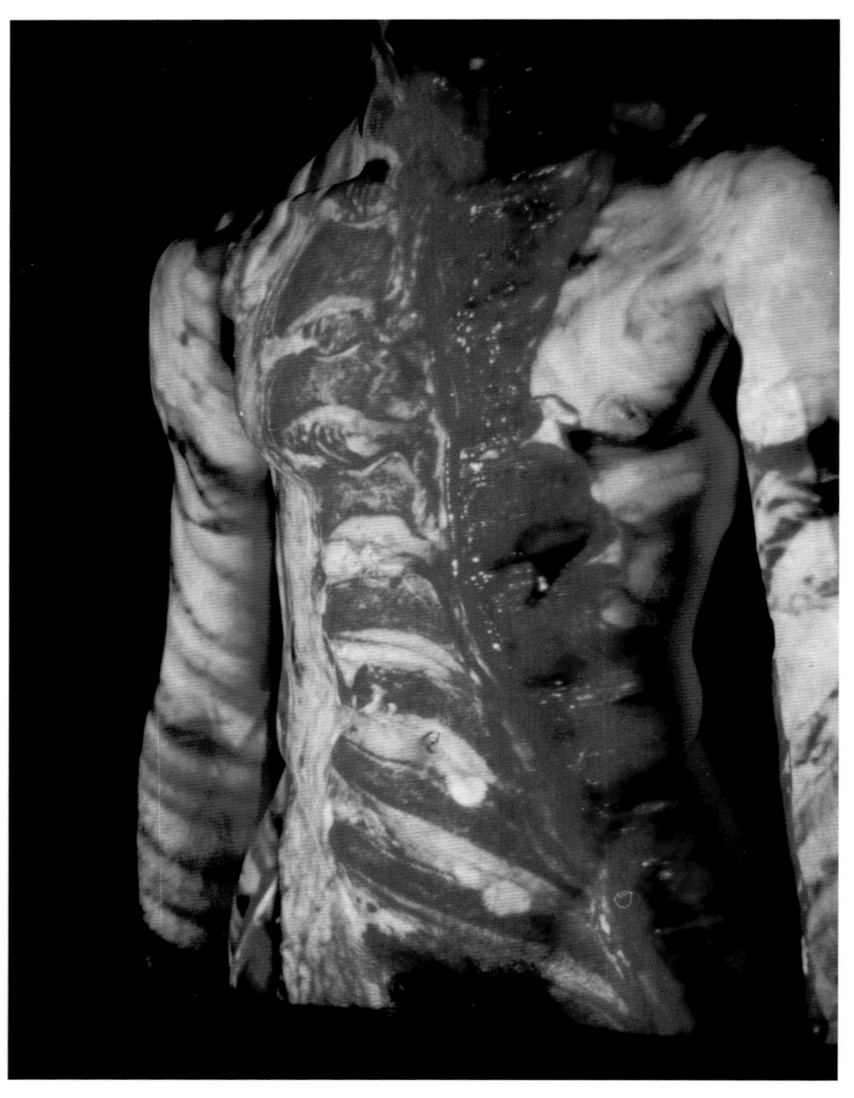

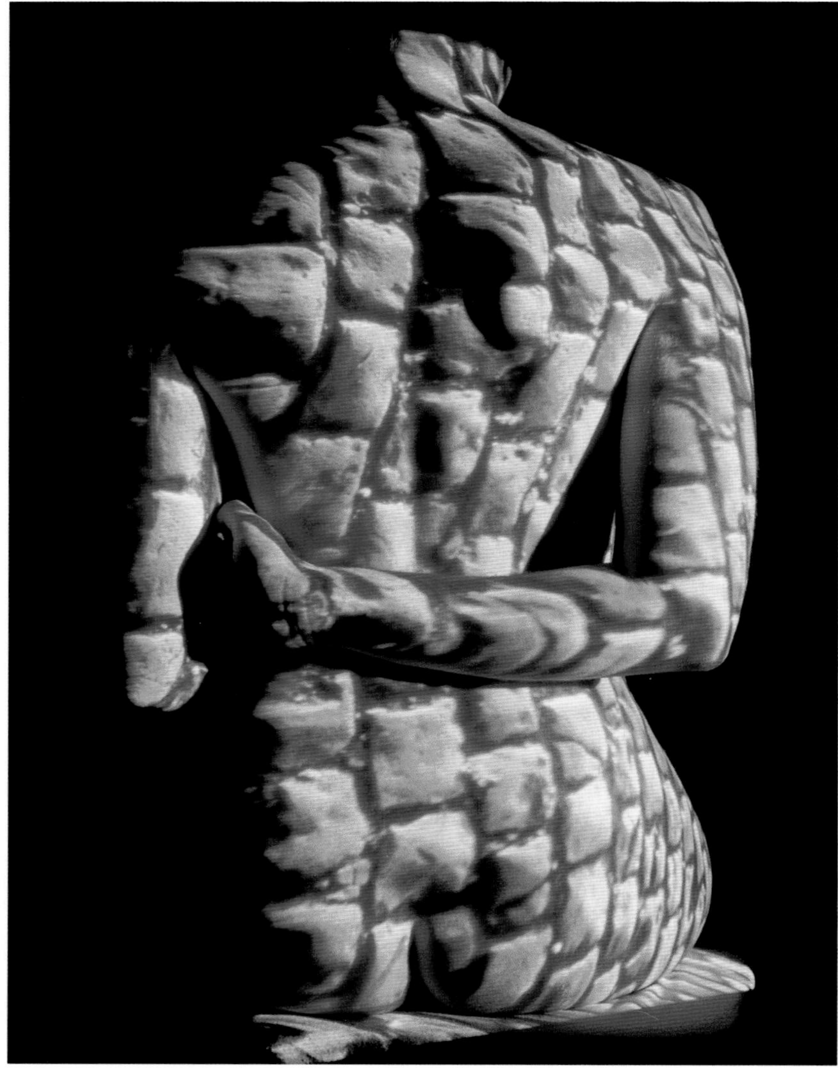

Michael Bertram

Katrin Nalop

Jo Kirchherr

Vadim Filimonov

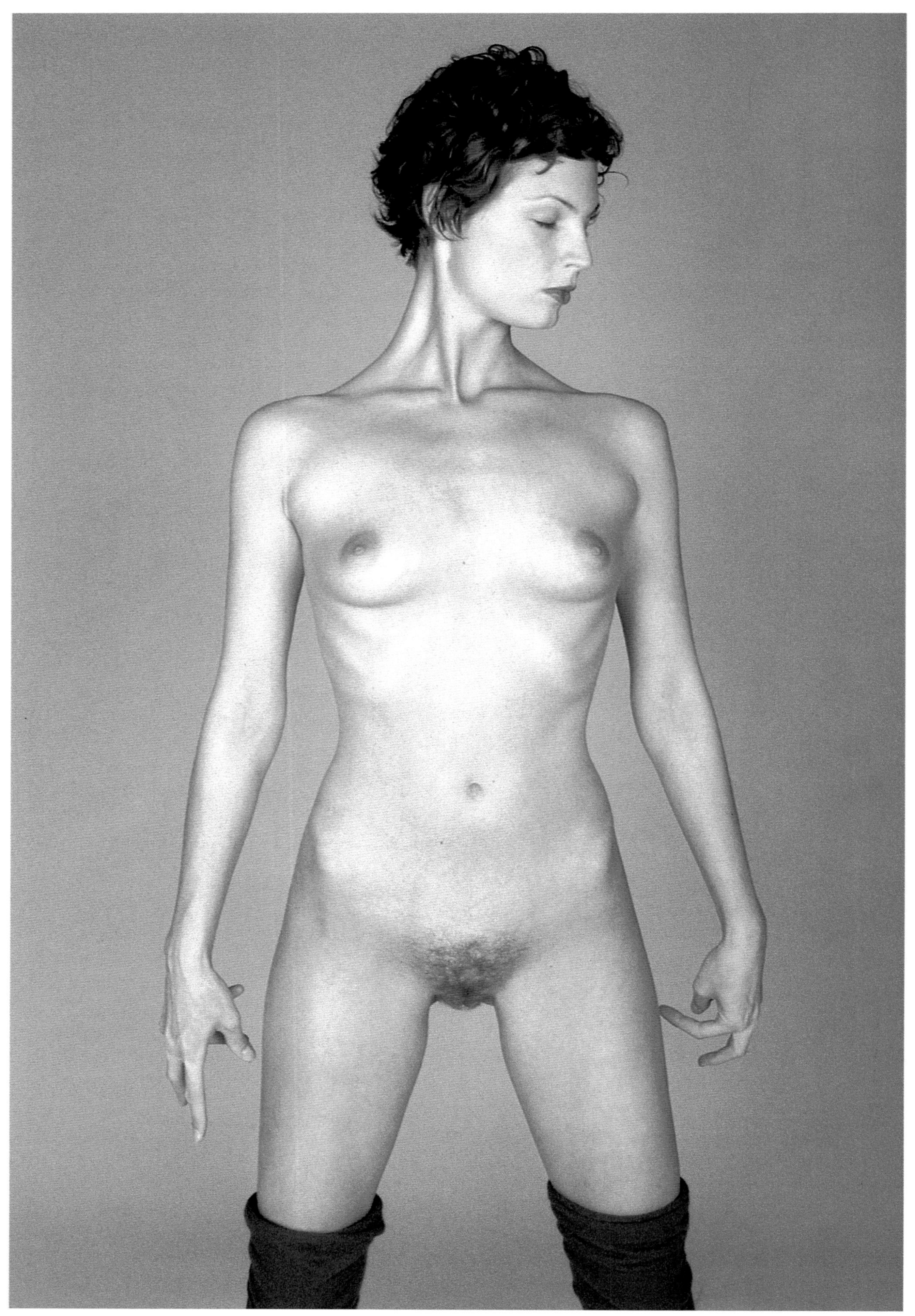

Michael Fitzthum

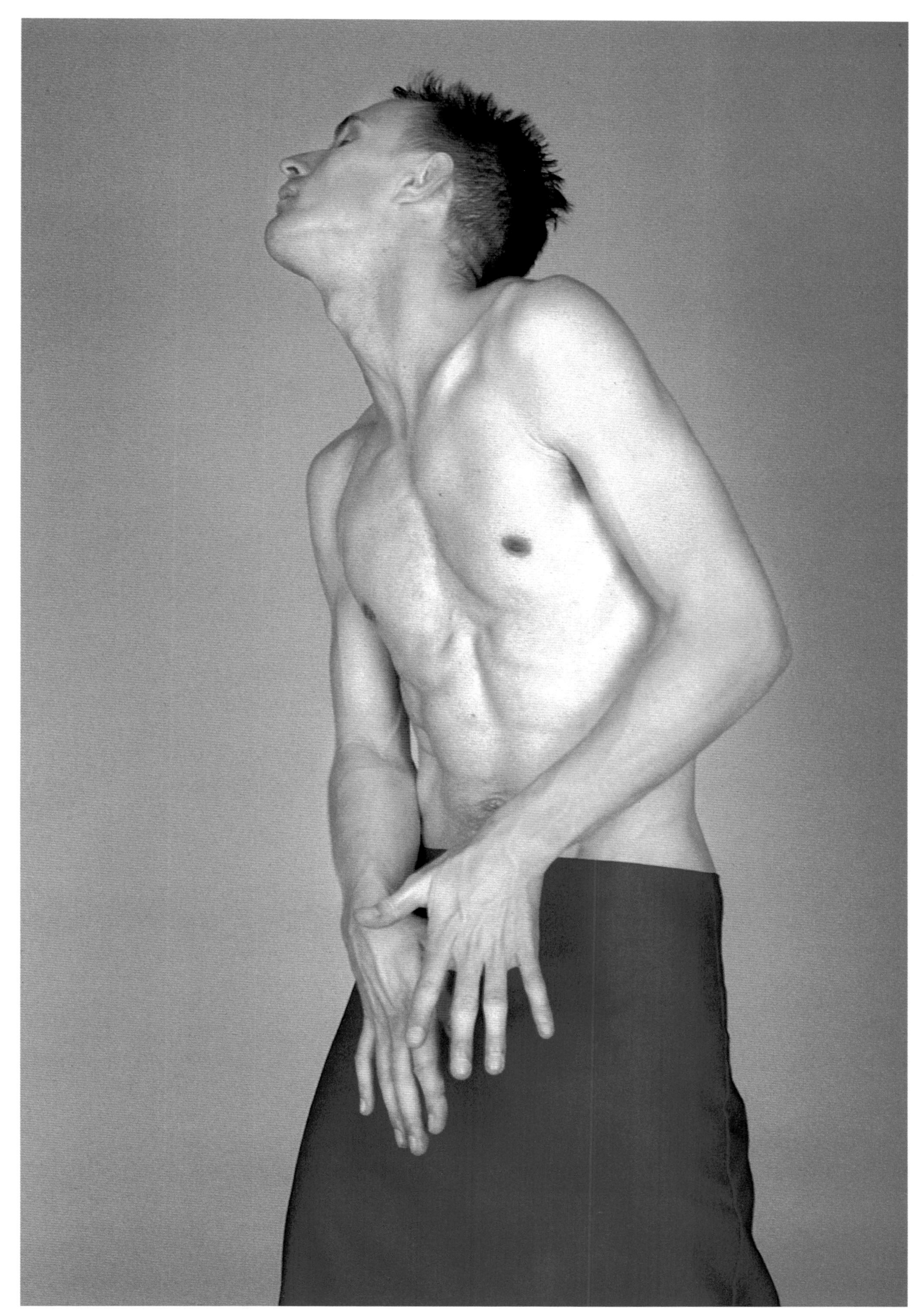

MALE II

Erwin Hartsuiker ▷

◀◀ Ed Freeman

Almond Chu

Martin Langhorst

Paul Walker

◄◄ Gerhard Vormwald

Sandra Scholz

Abilio Lope

Edgar Zippel

Kingdome 19 ▷

EXPOSITIONS
TOUCH
IF I WAS WEAK
FORGIVE ME
PECTUS

◀◀ Zefiro & Luna

Thorsten Eichhorst

FEMALE II

◀◀ Klaus-Peter Nordmann

Sabine Kühne

Felix Holzer

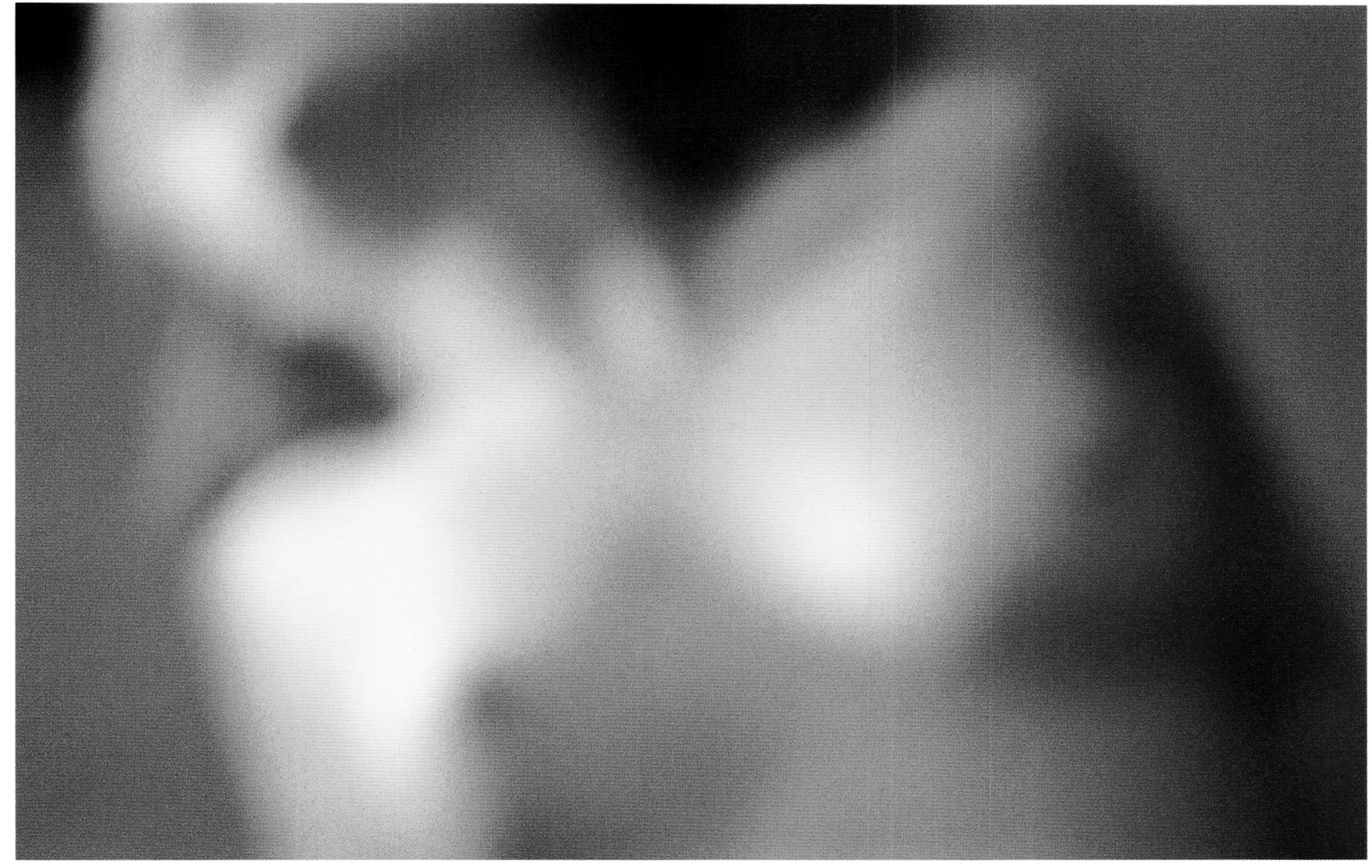

Felix Holzer

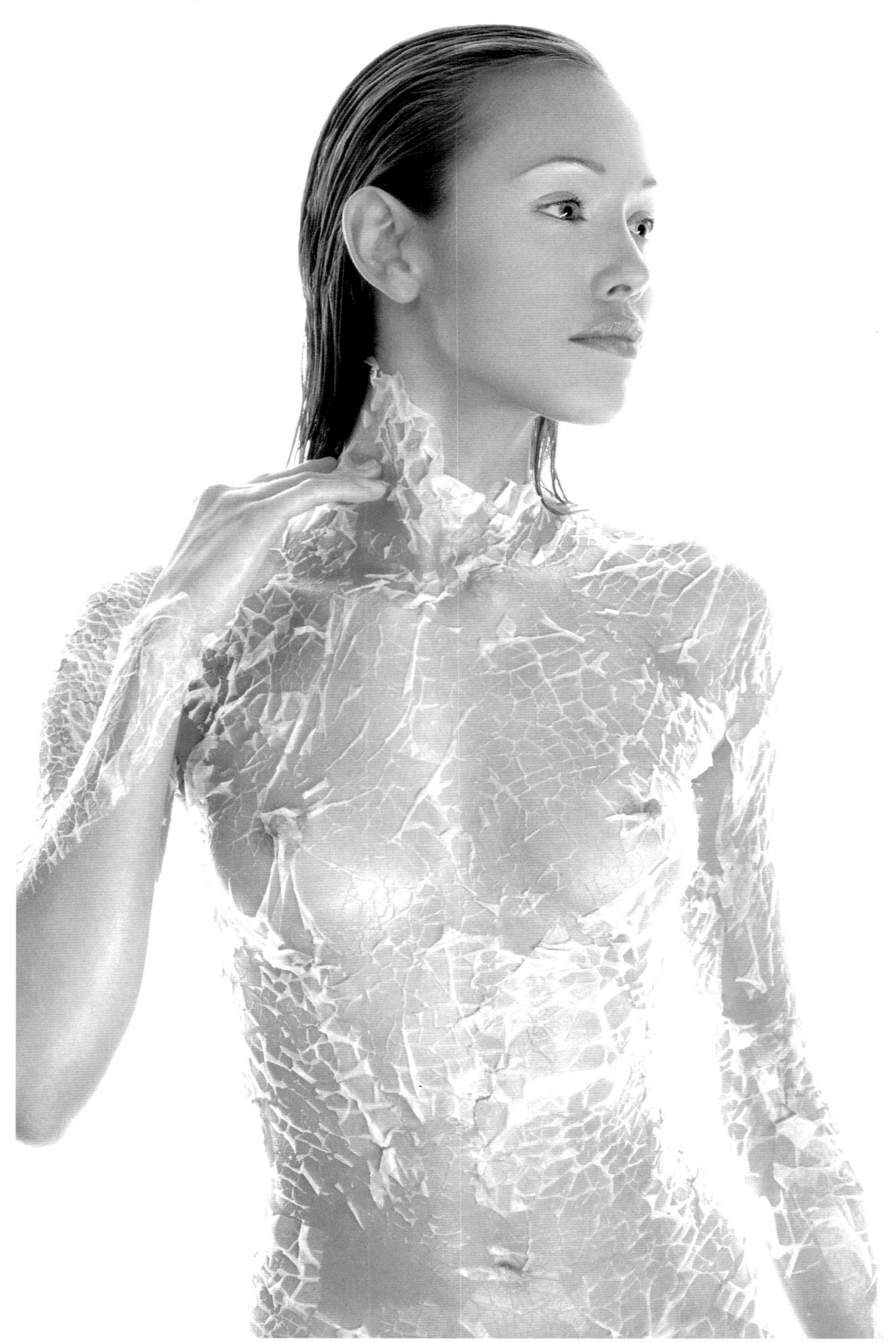

Klaus-Peter Nordmann

Jocelyne Moreau

Patrick Lhullier

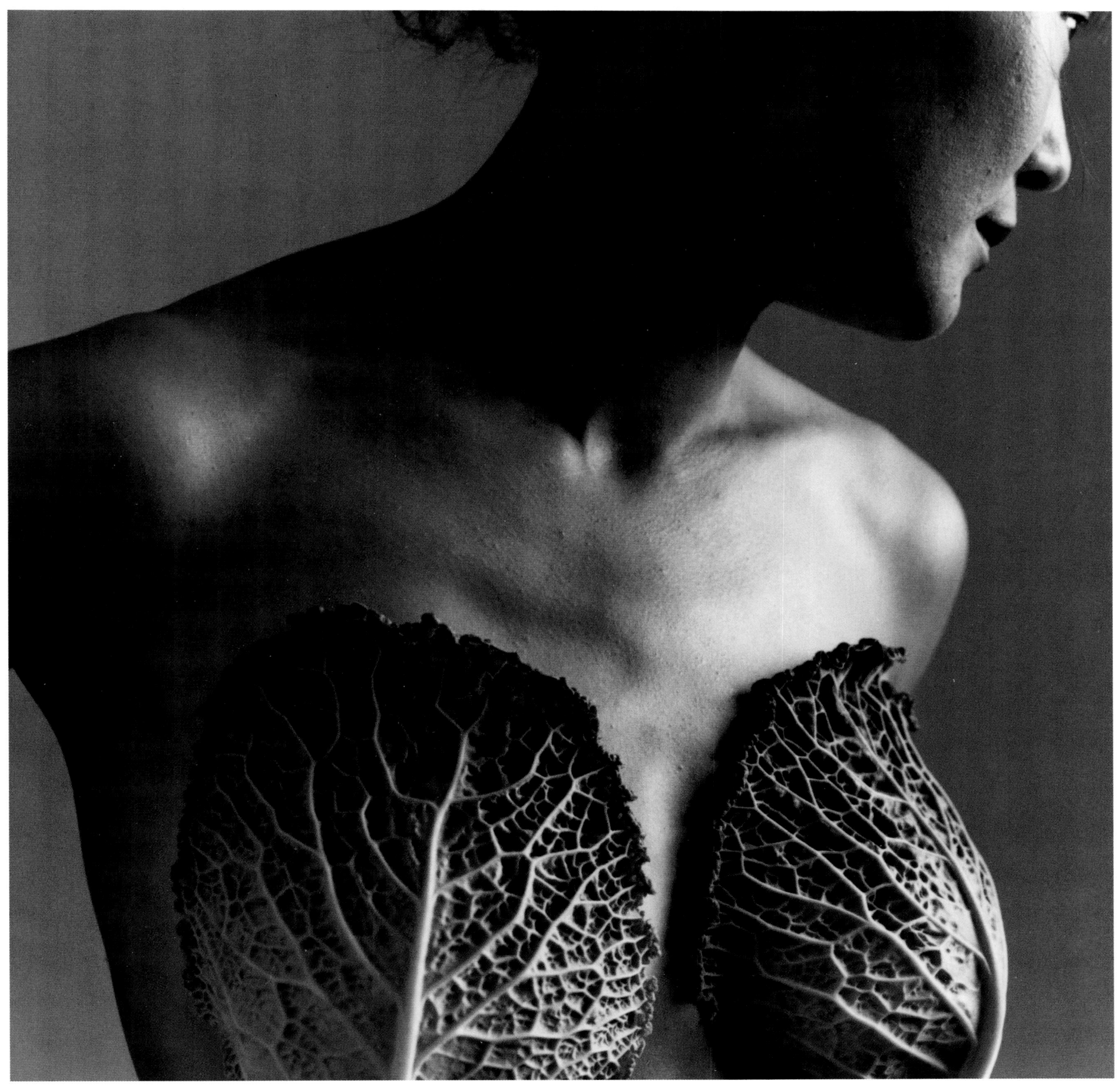

Jan Tepass

Tim Dry

Benny De Grove

Kim Christensen

Timoteo Dallessandro

Peter Dazeley

Jonnie Miles

◁ Kim Christensen

Fjodor C. Buis

Uwe Kiebel

◁ Tak Kojima

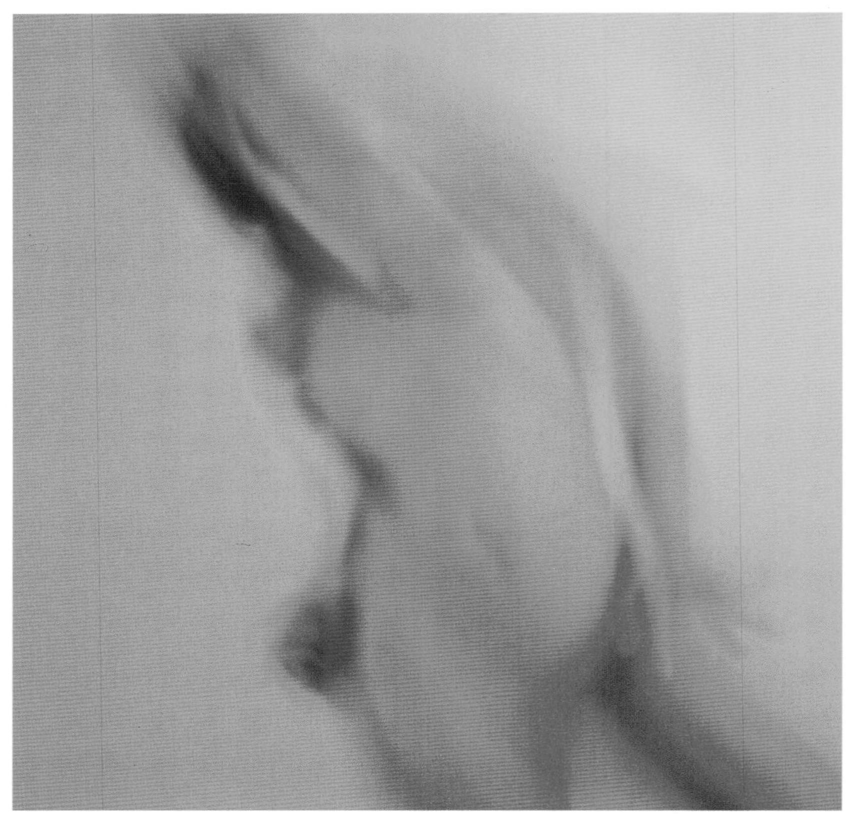

Kurt Paulus

Ralph Weber

Jo Kirchherr

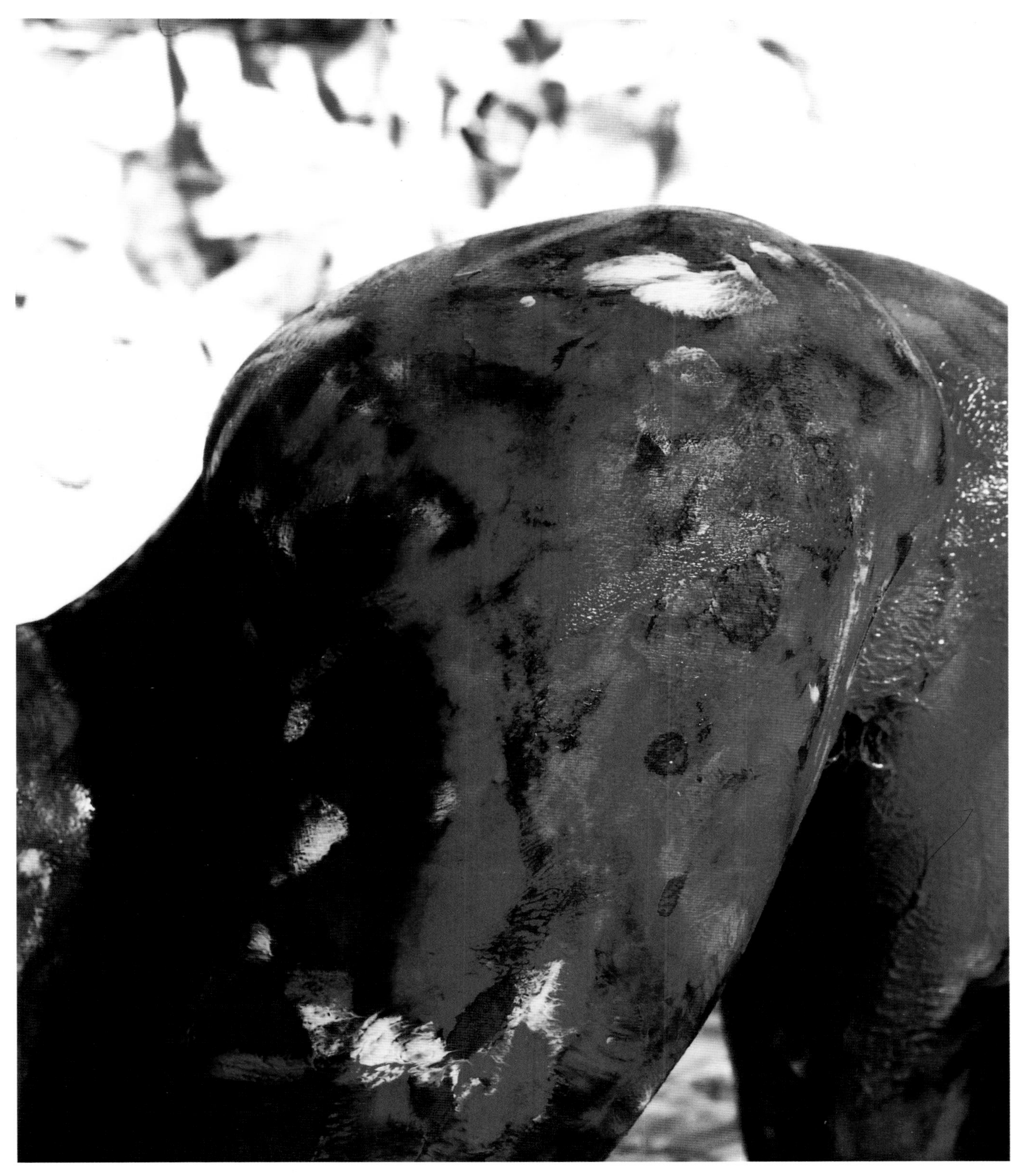

Stephan Hederich

Boris Schmalenberger

Franco Fontana

Wolfgang Eichler

Harald Köster

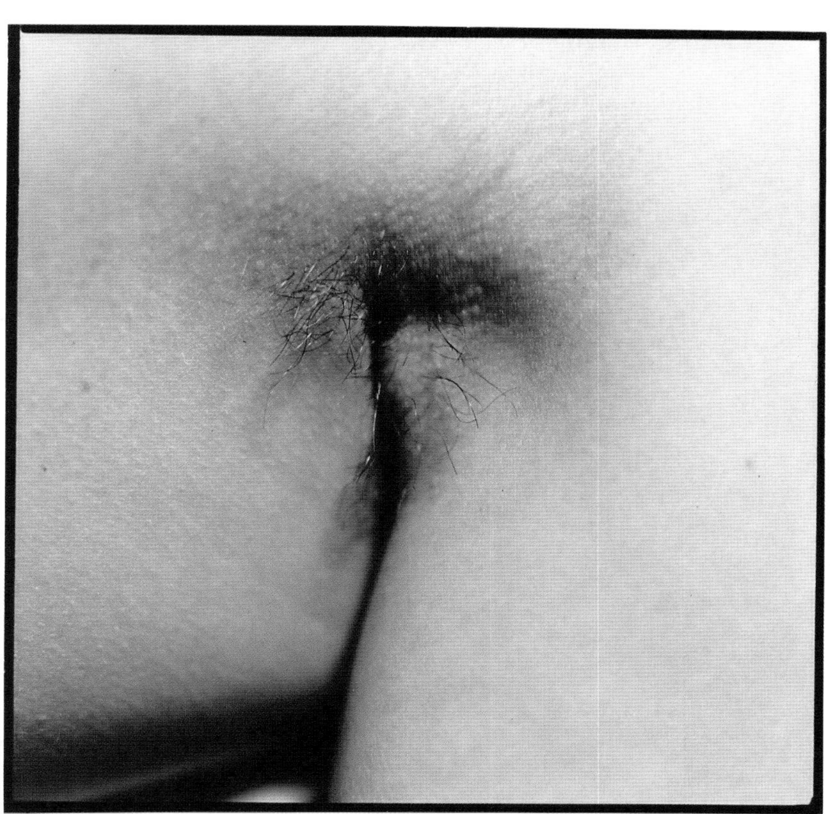

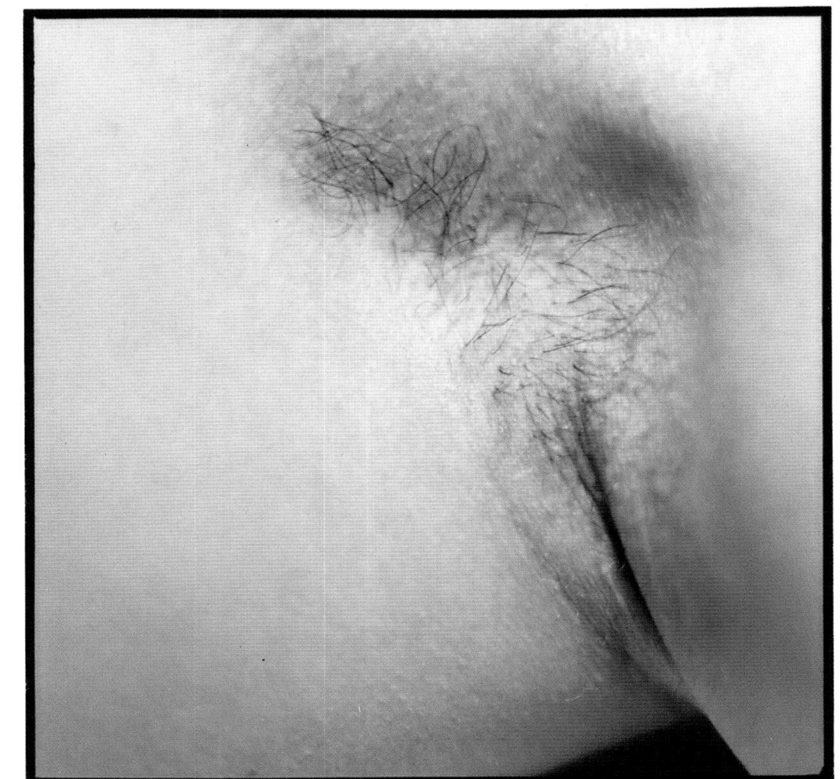

Mischa Haller

Wes Hardison

Klaus Bossemeyer

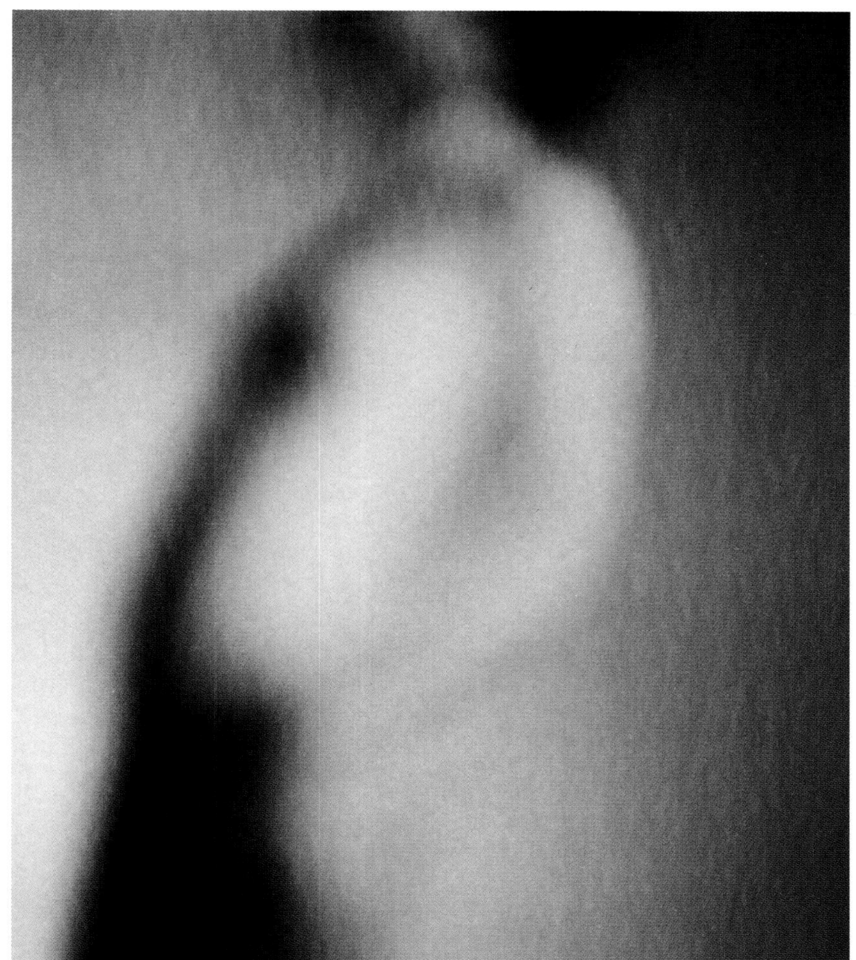

Ron Levine

Ebby May

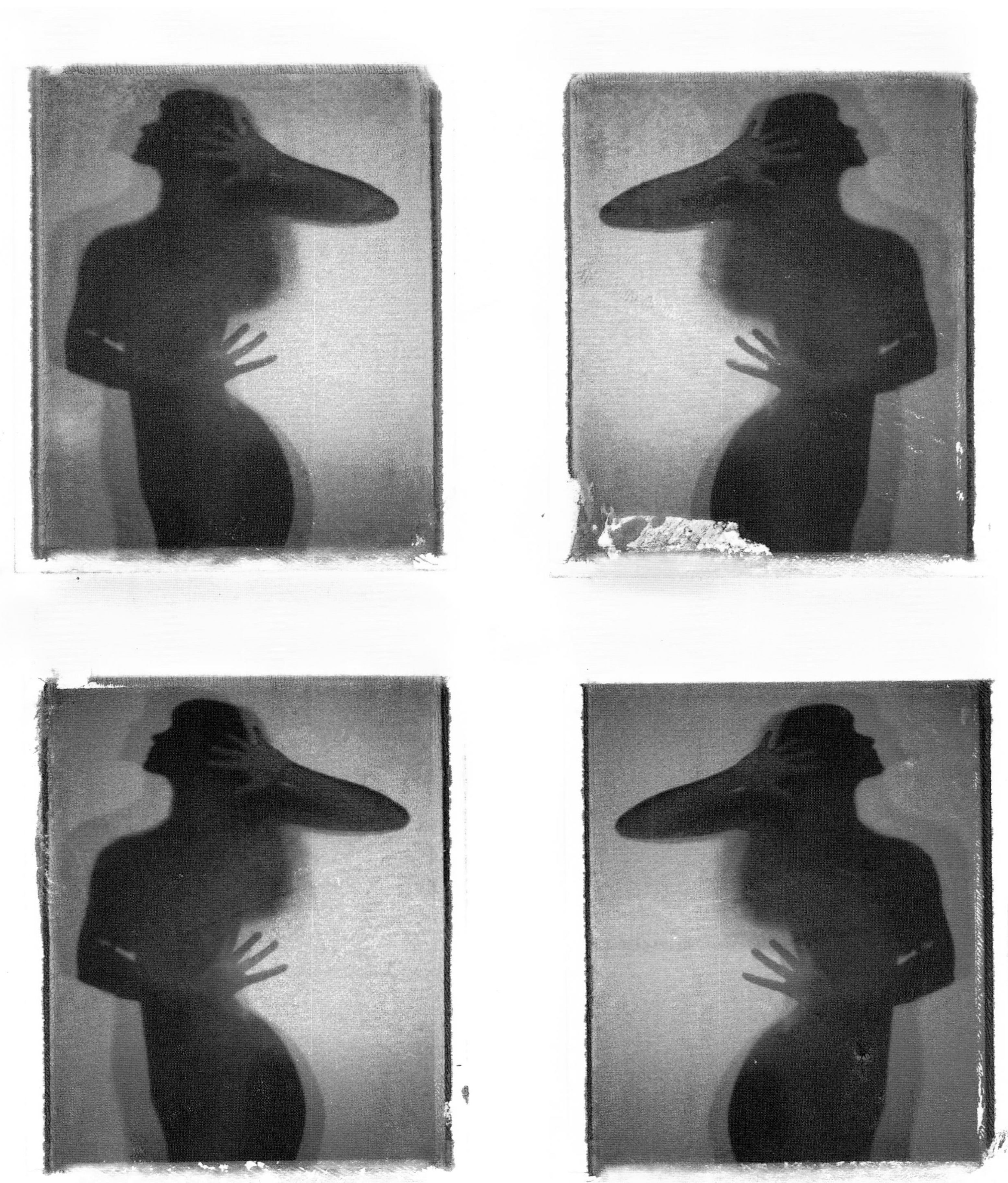

Graham Monro

Danny Conant

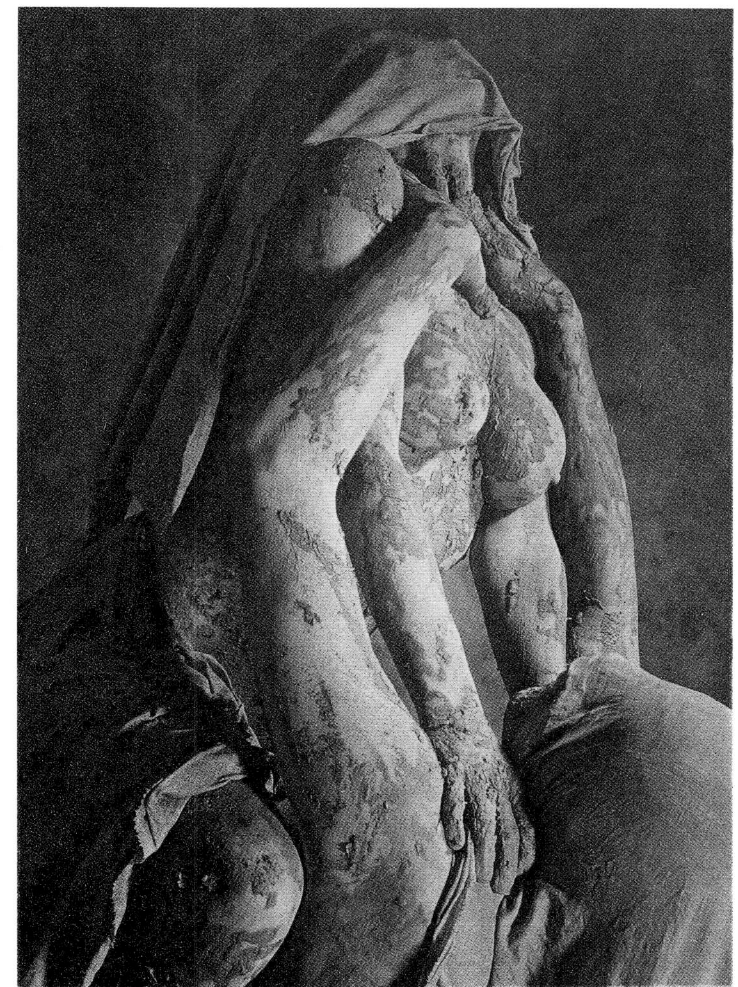

Claude Fauville

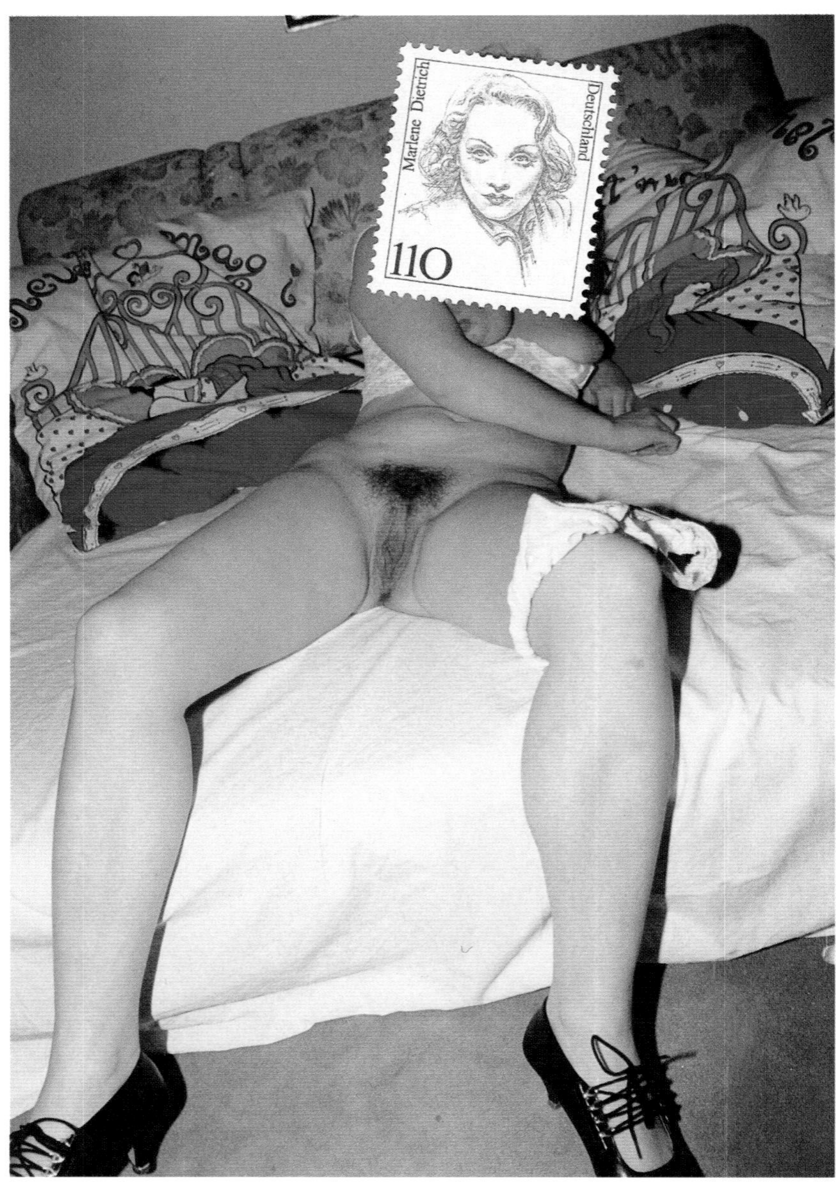

Ralph Bageritz

20
DEUTSCHE
DEMOKRATISCHE REPUBLIK

Susanne Amann

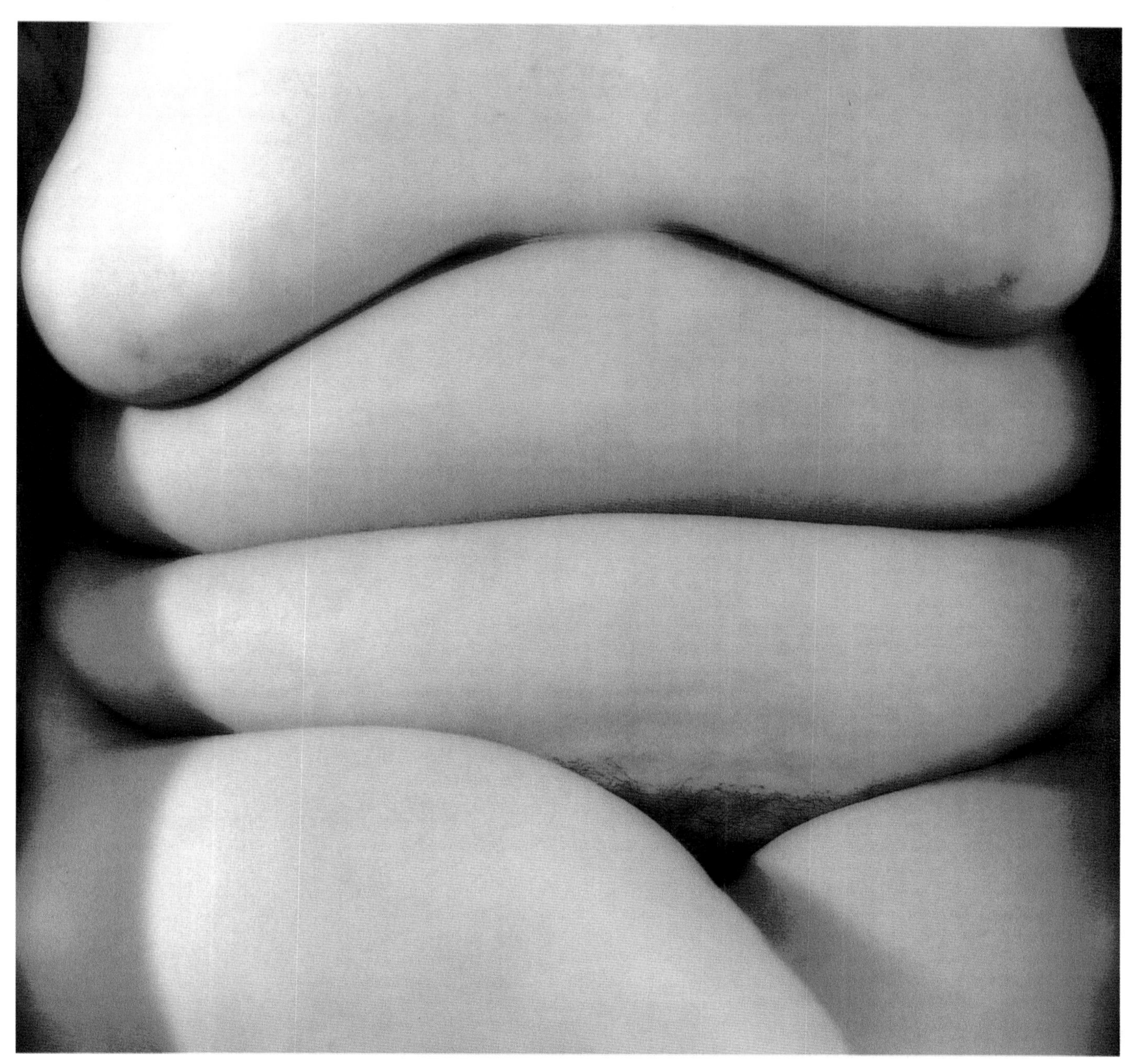

Wes Hardison

Ann Brown

Alva Bernadine

Alfons Iseli

H. H. Capor

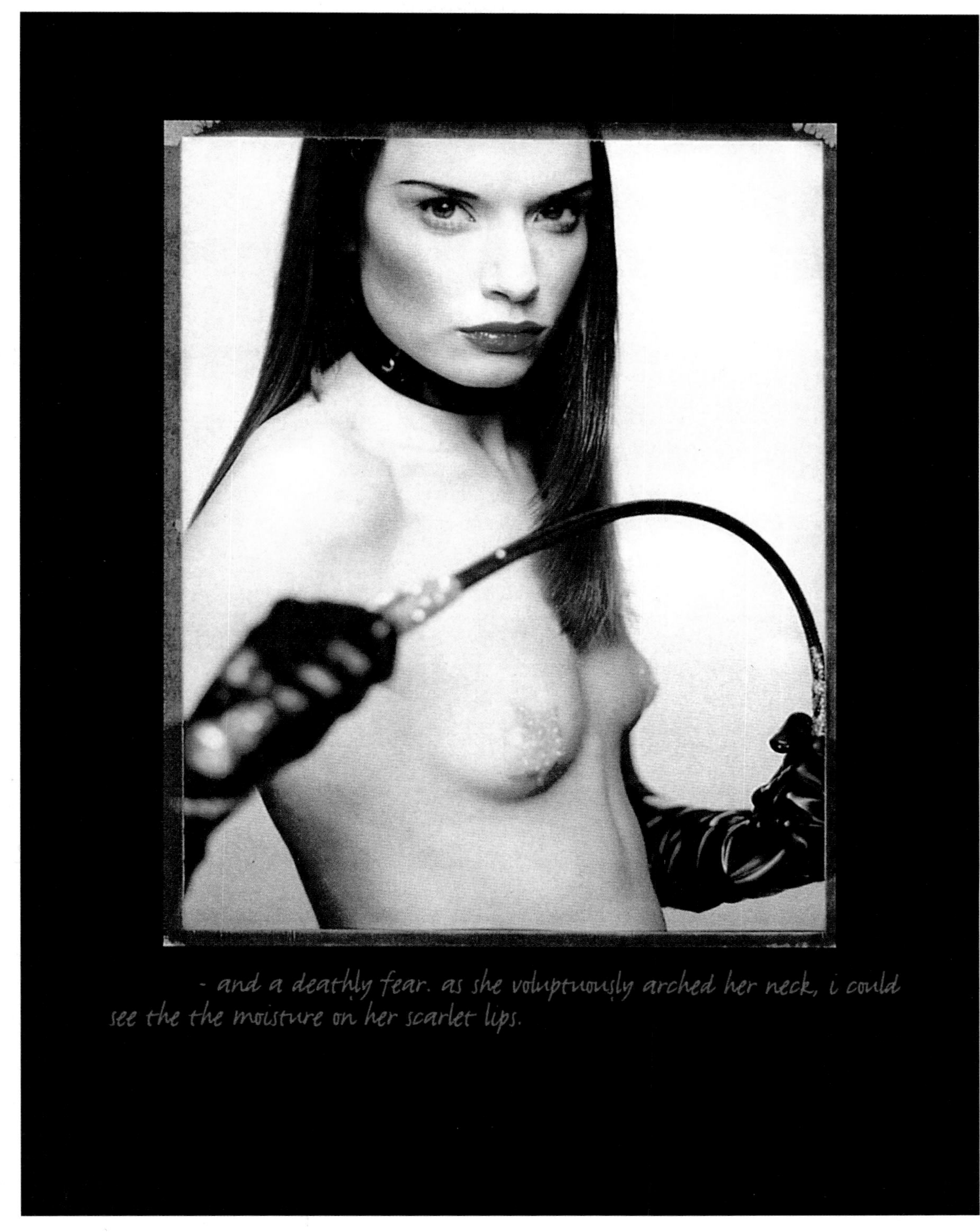
- and a deathly fear. as she voluptuously arched her neck, i could
see the the moisture on her scarlet lips.

Frank Peinemann

◁ Fred George

Abilio Lope

Uwe Kempen

Addresses

Peter Adler *146*
Friedrichstr. 44
10969 Berlin
Germany

Susanne Amann *222*
fotoart-Wiesner
Baumhackergasse 1
93047 Regensburg
Germany
Tel.: +49-941-56.57.99
Fax: +49-941-56.57.96
E-Mail: sue_susan@hotmail.com

Anderson & Low Photographers
96/97, 99
18D, Redcliffe Gardens,
London SW 10 9 EX
England
Tel./Fax: +44-171-351.26.01
Mobile: +44-956-24.73.00

Sergio Assabbi *51*
Uruguay 1292 22 „A“
1016 Capital Federal
Argentina
Tel./Fax: +54-11-48.11.76.36
c/o Cristina Nagengast
Tel.: +49-3941-61.20.10

Onofre Bachiller *134/135, 136*
C / Muntaner 128. 2°, 2a
080026 Barcelona
Spain
Tel./Fax: +34-93-649.18.34.53
E-Mail: onofre@wanadoo.es

Pascal Baetens *15, 34, 35*
W. Coosemanstraat 122
3010 Kessel-Lo
Belgium
Tel: +32-16-25.84.11
Fax: +32-16-25.84.70
Mobile: +32-75-39.02.44
E-Mail: ascal.baetens@advalvas.be

Ralph Bageritz *220, 221*
Ehrenstr. 23
50672 Köln
Germany
Tel./Fax: +49-221-25.57.13

Phil Bekker *44, 45*
5070 Trimble Road
Atlanta, GA 30342
USA
Tel./Fax: +1-404-688.59.97
E-Mail: bekker@bekker.com
Homepage: www.bekker.com

Alva Bernadine *77, 225*
23 Exbury House-Ferndale Road
London SW9 8AZ
England
Tel.: +44-171-326.42.77
Homepage:
www.bernadinism.demon.co.uk

Michael Bertram *150*
Miesenheimerstr. 4a
56637 Plaidt
Germany
Tel.: +49-2651-77125
Homepage:
www.kultur-boerse.de

Michael Bidner *116/117*
Mehringdamm 61
10961 Berlin
Germany
Tel.: +49-30-693.79.24

Markus Bollen *25 bottom*
Froschpfad 9
51422 Bensberg
Germany
Tel.: +49-2204-22220
Fax: +49-2204-67547
E-Mail: MarkBollen@aol.com

Xavier Bonnin *54, 55*
Pappelallee 6
10437 Berlin
Germany
Tel.: +49-30-441.73.76
Mobile: +49-172-535.63.15

Klaus Bossemeyer *211*
Goldbrink 32
48167 Münster
Germany
Tel.: +49-2506-69.29
Fax: +49-2506-60.59
Mobile: +49-172-404.14.14
E-Mail: bossemeyer-foto-text@
t-online.de

Richard Bradbury *52*
7a Langley Street
London WC2H 9JA
England
Tel.: +44-171-497.66.77
Fax: +44-171-497.66.88
E-mail: richardbradbury@msn.com
Homepage: rbradbury.com

Ann Brown *121, 224*
5623 Rockhill,
Kansas City, Missouri 64110
USA
Tel.: +1-816-333.52.01
E-Mail: superpea7@aol.com

Fjodor C. Buis *194, 195*
Vosmaerstraat 41
2032 La Haarlem
Netherlands
Tel.: +31-23-535.54.20
Fax: +31-23-536.61.00
Mobile: +31-23-536.61.00
E-Mail: Fjodor.Buis@inter.nl.net

Christoph Büschel *144, 145*
Bahnhofstr. 14
31812 Bad Pyrmont
Germany
Tel./Fax: +49-5281-60.69.71

H.H. Capor *227*
Grofler Ring 22
1130 Wien
Austria
Tel.: +43-1-802.51.71

Kim Christensen *188, 192*
KC-Photography
P.O. Box 47 216
Ponsonby, Auckland,
New Zealand
Tel./Fax: +64-9-817.67.73
Mobile: +64-25-97.08.37
E-Mail:
kcphotography@hotmail.com

Almond Chu *90, 93, 161*
RM 109, BLK. D
12 Oil Street, North Point
Hong Kong
China
Tel.: +86-852-25.30.35.83
Fax: +86-852-25.30.37.05

Danny S. Conant *218*
3901 Woodbine Street
Chevy Chase, Maryland 20815
USA
Tel.: +1-301-652.91.02
Fax: +1-301-652.44.79
E-Mail: danny@his.com
Homepage: www.dannyconant.com

Arnold Crane *22,23*
In focus Galerie am Dom
Marzellenstrafle, 9
50667 Köln
Germany
Tel./Fax: +49-221-130.03.41
Mobile: +49-177-320.29.13
E-Mail: galeriefoc@aol.com
Homepage: www.artistguide.com/
in_focus_galerie_am_dom.html

Timoteo Dallessandro *189*
Galaxy Contacts
c/o Buche
Argentinier Str. 36
1040 Wien
Austria
Tel.: +43-1-505.85.71
Tel.: +43-1-545.25.07

Michael Dannenmann *111*
Konkordiastr. 20
40219 Düsseldorf
Germany
Tel.: +49-211-30.80.99
Fax: +49-211-30.80.90

Peter Dazeley *58, 190, 191*
The Studios
5 Heathmans Road
Parsons Green
London SW6 4TJ
England
Tel.: +44-171-736.31.71
Fax: +44-171-371.88.76

Benny De Grove *187*
Fotostudio De Grove bvba
Zwijnaardse Steenweg 28a
9820 Merelbeke
Belgium
Tel.: +32-9-231.96.16
Fax: +32-9-231.95.94
Mobile: +32-7-564.96.11

Sinje Dillenkofer *137, 142, 143*
Fangelsbachstr. 30
70180 Stuttgart
Germany
Tel.: +49-711-640.60.66
Fax: +49-711-711-60.48.73
E-Mail: sinjed@aol.com

Yuri Dojc Inc. *14, 40, 41*
28 Briar Hill Avenue
Toronto, ON. M4R 1H6
Canada
Tel.: +1-416-481.46.48
Fax: +1-416-481.32.62
E-Mail: stop@yuridojc.com
Homepage: www.yuridojc.com

Nick Dolding *64*
28/29 Great Sutton Str.
London EC1V 0DS
England
Tel.: +44-171-490.24.54

Alexander Döring *67*
Köpenickerstr. 41
10179 Berlin
Germany
Tel.: +49-30-27.59.11.70
E-Mail: gemuese@zedat.fu-berlin.de

Tim Dry *186*
Impresaria International
4th floor, 25-27 Oxford St.
London W1R 1RF
England
Tel.: +44-171-287.79.90
Fax: +44-171-287.79.63
E-Mail: Impressaria@dial.webs.co.uk

Rafael Navarro *24*
In focus Galerie am Dom
Marzellenstr. 9
50667 Köln
Germany
Tel./Fax: +49-221-130.03.41
Mobile: +49-177-320.29.13
E-Mail: galeriefoc@aol.com
Homepage: www.artistguide.com/
in_focus_galerie_am_dom.html

Dan Nelken *128, 129*
43 West 27 Street
New York, NY 10001
USA
Tel.: +1-212-532.74.71
Fax: +1-212-532.93.81
E-Mail: dnelkeninc@aol.com

Klaus-Peter Nordmann *176, 182*
Weissenburgstr. 8
65183 Wiesbaden
Germany
Tel.: +49-611-40.93.69
Fax: +49-611-40.76.02
Homepage: www.kpnordmann.de

Michael E. Northrup *147*
1900 Eutaw Place
Baltimore, MD 21217
USA
Tel/Fax: +1-410-669.47.05
E-Mail:
strobo@qis.net
strobo@strobophoto.com
Homepage: www.strobophoto.com

Kurt Paulus Photography *198, 199*
Blumenthalstr. 7
90429 Nürnberg
Germany
Tel.: +49-911-26.55.50
Fax: +49-911-26.69.59

Frank Peinemann *229*
Maastrichter Str. 49
50672 Köln
Germany
Tel.: +49-221-510.41.89
Fax: +49-221-510.42.91
Mobile: +49-172-202.96.00

Ansgar Pudenz/Rusch *140, 141*
Elke Froschauer „represented by“
Agentur für Fotografen,
Körnerstr. 2 RGB
80469 München
Germany
Tel.: +49-89-74.68.98.14
Fax: +49-89-74.68.98.15

Renata Ratajczyk *88, 89*
Light Vision
323 Rusholme Road, # 1403
Toronto, ON. M6H 2Z2
Canada
Tel.: +1-416-538.10.87
Fax: +1-416-533.95.69
E-Mail:
renatara@ica.net
Renatara@hotmail.com
Homepage:
www.ncphoto.com/lightvision
www.virtualcolony.com/renatar

Regina Recht *104, 105*
Keno Studio
Lindwurmstr. 145
80337 München
Germany
Tel.: +49-89-747.01.35
Fax: +49-89-747.07.35

Frank Rheinboldt *30, 31, 102*
18, bd. Voltaire
75011 Paris
France
Tel.: +33-1-43.57.96.57

João Fernando Romão Días da Silva *86*
R. João das Regras, no. 6-1P
2750 Cascais
Portugal
Tel./Fax: +351-1-483.10.84

Hisako Sakurai *28, 29*
1-26-5 Kakinokizaka, Meguro-ku
Tokyo 152-0022
Japan
Tel./Fax: +81-3-37.17.03.22
E-Mail: hisako23@bd.mbn.or.jp
Homepage: plaza19.mbn.or.jp/
Sakurai23bwphoto

Anne Marie von Sarosdy
37, 103, 122, 124, 138
Pionierstr. 51
40215 Düsseldorf
Germany
Tel.: +49-211-385.75.75
Fax: +49-211-385.75.73
E-Mail: sarosdy@aol.com
Homepage:
www.selectonline.com/sarosdy

Thomas Schlömann *20, 48*
Präsident-Krahn-Str. 8
22765 Hamburg
Germany
Tel.: +49-40-389.47.35
Mobile: +49-171-171.91.17

Boris Schmalenberger *204*
Müllerstr. 6
70199 Stuttgart
Germany
Tel.: +49-711-640.54.07
Fax: +49-711-640.54.08
Mobile: +49-171-416.65.14

Sandra Scholz *168*
fotoart-Wiesner
Baumhackergasse 1
Germany
Tel.: +49-941-56.57.99
Fax: +49-941-56.57.96
E-Mail: sue_susan@hotmail.com

Jürgen Schulzki *32/33*
Fotografie Elsner/Schulzki
Hermann-Löns-Str. 7
51469 Bergisch-Gladbach
Germany
Tel.: +49-2202-50941
Fax: +49-2202-56720

Mark Smith *21*
S. Marco 3420
3014 Venice
Italy
Tel.: +39-41-522.39.60
Fax: +39-41-523.96.36
E-Mail: msmith@tin.it

Josef Snobl *11, 12/13*
Wissmannstr. 1a
50823 Köln
Germany
Tel.: +49-221-51.18.71
Fax: +49-221-510.32.79

Catherine Steinmann *63*
Park Avenue 1185
New York, NY 10128
USA
Tel.: +1-212-831.95.07
Fax: +1-212-410.21.67
Homepage:
www.catherinesteinmann.com

Brigitte Tast *53*
Lasseweg 4
31174 Schellerten
Germany
Tel.: +49-5123-43.30
Fax: +49-5123-20.15

Jan Tepass *57, 92, 185*
Parkgürtel 31
50823 Köln
Germany
Tel./Fax: +49-221-55.24.15

Benno Thoma *94, 120*
Nicolaas Beetsstr. 29
7514 CV Enschede
Netherlands
Tel./Fax: +31-53-432.74.76

Kimikazu Tomizawa *26, 27*
2-1-13 Koishikawa,Bunkyo-Ku,
Kōrakuen View Hight #308
Tokyo
Japan
Tel./Fax: +81-3-58.02.53.63

Barbara Traub *108, 109*
588 Sutter St. PMB 308
San Francisco, CA 94102
USA
Tel./Fax: +1-415-922.88.11
E-Mail: btraub@well.com
Homepage:
www.zpub.com/mediaz/btraub.html

Vesselin Valtchev *82, 83*
Obektiv, Studio
9151 Kichevo/Varna
Bulgaria
Tel./Fax: +359-52-67.33.20

Michael Vana *41, 70*
Am Schwarzenberg 33
97078 Würzburg
Germany
Tel.: +49-931-28.25.14
Mobile: +49-172-861.42.03

Gerhard Vormwald *71, 164, 165*
52, rue Pernety
75014 Paris
France
Tel.: +33-1-45.43.11.67
Fax: +33-1-40.44.79.98

Paul Walker *166, 167*
Event Horizon Photography
145 Farrell Street
Port Melbourne
Victoria 3207
Australia
Tel.: +61-3-96.46.92.81
Fax: +61-3-96.46.99.04
Mobile: +61-412-61.78.61
E-Mail: walkers@netspace.net.au

Ralph Weber *56, 200/201*
Photographenagentur Fabio
Tripicchio
Hans-Bunte-Str. 13
79108 Freiburg
Germany
Tel.: +49-761-556.95.90
Fax: +49-761-556.95.92
E-Mail: tripicchio@hotmail.com

George Wieser *36*
35 Great Jones St.
New York, NY 10012
USA
Tel.: +1-212-505.64.04
Fax: +1-212-533.46.36

Elisabeth Wiesner *112, 113*
foto art
Baumhackergasse 1
93047 Regensburg
Germany
Tel.: +49-941-56.57.99
Fax: +49-941-56-57.96
E-Mail: scheiner@donau.de

Hildegard M. Wilms *62*
Körnerstr. 94-96
50823 Köln
Germany
Tel.: +49-221-510.71.77
Fax: +49-221-510.28.42
E-Mail: INFO@gilda.de
Homepage: www.gilda.de